GETTING A BUSINESS LOAN

FINANCING YOUR MAIN STREET BUSINESS

Ty Kiisel

Apress

Getting a Business Loan: Financing Your Main Street Business

ISBN-13 (pbk): 978-1-4302-4998-6

ISBN-13 (electronic): 978-1-4302-4999-3

President and Publisher: Paul Manning
Acquisitions Editor: Jeff Olson
Editorial Board: Steve Anglin, Mark Beckner, Ewan Buckingham, Gary Cornell,
    Louise Corrigan, James DeWolf, Jonathan Gennick, Jonathan Hassell,
    Robert Hutchinson, Michelle Lowman, James Markham, Matthew Moodie,
    Jeff Olson, Jeffrey Pepper, Douglas Pundick, Ben Renow-Clarke,
    Dominic Shakeshaft, Gwenan Spearing, Matt Wade, Steve Weiss, Tom Welsh
Coordinating Editor: Rita Fernando
Copy Editor: Kezia Endsley
Compositor: SPi Global
Indexer: SPi Global
Cover Designer: Anna Ishchenko

Distributed to the book trade worldwide by Springer Science+Business Media New York, 233 Spring Street, 6th Floor, New York, NY 10013. Phone 1-800-SPRINGER, fax (201) 348-4505, e-mail orders-ny@springer-sbm.com, or visit www.springeronline.com. Apress Media, LLC is a California LLC and the sole member (owner) is Springer Science + Business Media Finance Inc (SSBM Finance Inc). SSBM Finance Inc is a Delaware corporation.

For information on translations, please e-mail rights@apress.com, or visit www.apress.com.

Apress and friends of ED books may be purchased in bulk for academic, corporate, or promotional use. eBook versions and licenses are also available for most titles. For more information, reference our Special Bulk Sales–eBook Licensing web page at www.apress.com/bulk-sales.

Any source code or other supplementary materials referenced by the author in this text is available to readers at www.apress.com. For detailed information about how to locate your book's source code, go to www.apress.com/source-code/.

Apress Business: The Unbiased Source of Business Information

Apress business books provide essential information and practical advice, each written for practitioners by recognized experts. Busy managers and professionals in all areas of the business world—and at all levels of technical sophistication—look to our books for the actionable ideas and tools they need to solve problems, update and enhance their professional skills, make their work lives easier, and capitalize on opportunity.

Whatever the topic on the business spectrum—entrepreneurship, finance, sales, marketing, management, regulation, information technology, among others—Apress has been praised for providing the objective information and unbiased advice you need to excel in your daily work life. Our authors have no axes to grind; they understand they have one job only—to deliver up-to-date, accurate information simply, concisely, and with deep insight that addresses the real needs of our readers.

It is increasingly hard to find information—whether in the news media, on the Internet, and now all too often in books—that is even-handed and has your best interests at heart. We therefore hope that you enjoy this book, which has been carefully crafted to meet our standards of quality and unbiased coverage.

We are always interested in your feedback or ideas for new titles. Perhaps you'd even like to write a book yourself. Whatever the case, reach out to us at editorial@apress.com and an editor will respond swiftly. Incidentally, at the back of this book, you will find a list of useful related titles. Please visit us at www.apress.com to sign up for newsletters and discounts on future purchases.

The Apress Business Team

To the Main Street business owners who create the jobs and keep our local communities alive

Contents

Preface

I've spent the 30 or so years of my career in small business. Most of that time has been spent working with the Main Street–type businesses that feed us, do our dry cleaning, service our automobiles, and perform dozens of other services. Largely underappreciated, these Main Street businesses create the lion's share of new jobs and employ about half of the workforce in the United States.

Although politicians and community leaders like to laud the achievements of the successful business leaders within their communities, it sometimes feels like the deck is stacked against them. Ask any small business owner, and he or she will likely acknowledge that access to capital is one of the biggest challenges they face every day.

Recent years have been tough for everyone. Since the financial meltdown, subsequent recession, and the plodding recovery, our friends on Main Street have taken a beating. Regulators, along with an overall tightening of credit, have made it difficult for business people to find the capital they need to grow, hire employees, and strengthen local communities. What's more, many risk-averse bankers have even moved upstream to what they claim are more profitable customers, leaving the businesses that have traditionally relied on them as a vital part of the Main Street business community out in the cold.

It hasn't been that long ago that a small business owner could walk into the bank with an opportunity and walk out with the financing to make it a reality—those days are gone. Credit score, time in business, annual revenues, and collateral rule the day. Bankers want perfect borrowers. Unfortunately, most of us aren't perfect.

Fortunately for small business owners, there are still community banks and other non-bank lenders still interested in helping Main Street thrive and grow. You simply need to know where to look. This book should help.

About the Author

Ty Kiisel is a small business evangelist and veteran of over 30 years in the trenches of Main Street business. Kiisel writes about small business and small business financing for Lendio (www.lendio.com). Known for making best practices, tips, and advice easy to understand by weaving personal experiences and other anecdotes into relevant conversations about small business, Kiisel is a popular contributor to Forbes.com, The Business Fuel Podcast, and other industry publications.

Acknowledgments

It would have been impossible to finish this work without the support of my wife Sue. Her encouragement and support made it easy to devote the time required to finish. I also need to thank my editor Jeff Olson for his help, advice, and support. He always seemed to know just the right thing to say to help move the book along.

I would be remiss if I didn't acknowledge the work of Brock Blake and my colleagues at Lendio, who spend every day helping small business owners find the financing they need to fuel their American Dream. It's a great pleasure to be engaged in such a worthy endeavor.

Introduction

Looking back, there were many times early in my career when the information in this book would have been invaluable as I struggled to fund my Main Street business ambitions. Hopefully, this will help you fuel yours.

In the first few chapters, I talk about finding the right bank and the right banker. I explain what to look for and how to foster the kind of relationship that gives loan officers a reason to make small business loan decisions based upon something more than your credit score. I'm a big supporter of the role community banks play within the Main Street business infrastructure. Although their numbers are dwindling, there are still many looking to partner with the small business community in their community to build strong local economies.

No discussion on small business lending would be complete without mentioning the Small Business Administration (SBA), which you can find in Chapter 5 of this book. Although the SBA loan guarantee program might not be the biggest source of small business capital, it is an important source and accounts for approximately $30 billion annually.

The remaining chapters discuss equity funding sources, like angels and venture capital, and other options like factoring, the merchant cash advance, and specialty loan products designed specifically for small business owners.

If you've been into the bank and been turned down for a small business loan, you're not alone. But you still have options. In this book, you learn what those options are, where to find them, and how to evaluate if they're right for you and your small business. Over the last few years, non-traditional or alternative lenders have done a great job of filling the vacuum left behind by banks looking for greener pastures. As more and more such lenders enter the market, interest rates will continue to come down with the increased competition. Anything that makes access to capital easier for Main Street should be considered a good thing.

Regardless, if you persist in your quest for growth capital or simply want a solid line of credit to help you plug the cash shortfalls all businesses experience, you will find the money you need. As you'll see, some deals are better than others, and some—the ones to avoid—are too good to be true. And there'll be trade-offs regarding fees, collateral, and interest rates. Use this book to uncover options and don't give up. That's the American business spirit. Good luck!

Funding the American Dream

10 Percent Just Isn't Good Enough

Every day, Main Street business owners wrestle with the challenges of finding the cash they need to finance growth or to use as working capital. Banks want a credit score of 720, three to five good years in business, and a fat savings account.

My small business career started as a 16-year-old driving the delivery truck for my father's small industrial supply business. "If I had that," he would say about the banker's requirements, "I wouldn't need a business loan."

Financing a Main Street business isn't easy. Only 10% of loan applications made at the bank actually get approved, making it difficult for many small business owners to thrive and grow. Ironically, politicians like to talk about how important small business is to the economy. They just don't put their money where their mouths are.

In fairness to Uncle Sam, part of the problem is how the government defines exactly what makes up a small business. What the Small Business Administration (SBA) defines as a small business and what you and I might describe as a small business are likely not the same thing.

What Is a Small Business?

This is how the SBA[1] defines a small business:

- *Manufacturing*: Maximum number of employees may range from 500 to 1,500, depending on the type of product manufactured.

- *Wholesaling*: Maximum number of employees may range from 100 to 500, depending on the particular product being provided.

- *Services*: Annual receipts may not exceed $2.5 to $21.5 million, depending on the particular product being provided.

- *Retailing*: Annual receipts may not exceed $5.0 to $21.0 million, depending on the particular product being provided.

- *General and heavy construction*: General construction annual receipts may not exceed $13.5 to $17 million, depending on the type of construction.

- *Special trade construction*: Annual receipts may not exceed $7 million.

- *Agriculture*: Annual receipts may not exceed $0.5 to $9.0 million, depending on the agricultural product.

No wonder it's so confusing. I've spent the last 30 or so years of my career in small business. I've worked in organizations with half a dozen or so employees in addition to a software company with over 240 employees. They were both very different animals; the latter felt more like a big business to me. Yet, the SBA considers them both "small" businesses.

Although I don't want to get into an argument over semantics, I'm convinced that when politicians are on the news talking about how they want to help small business, they aren't talking about the same folks you and I think of as small businesses or small business owners.

My first job in a small business, working with my dad, was decidedly different from working in a software company with nearly 250 employees.

Most of us identify with the small businesses on Main Street—the local restaurant, the barbershop around the corner, the dry cleaner, and the local plumber. Main Street businesses are decidedly different from the

---

[1]http://www.sba.gov/content/what-sbas-definition-small-business-concern

multimillion-dollar software company or widget manufacturer in the office building or industrial park off the freeway, even though they may have started out as small businesses.

Why Does Main Street Matter?

Collectively, Main Street hires a lot of people.

Although Main Street may not be the biggest employer in your area, or in the nation for that matter, collectively a lot of people depend on small businesses for jobs. That's why politicians like to talk about small business owners so much.

When they talk about small businesses, what they really should be talking about is job creation, which is where small businesses really shine.

A 2010 study conducted by the National Bureau of Economic Research, "Who Creates Jobs? Small vs. Large vs. Young,"[2] suggests, "The younger companies are, the more jobs they create, regardless of their size."

With that in mind, I find it ironic, from a jobs-creation standpoint, that although they are at the very fountain of job creation (something that politicians on both sides of the aisle claim they want to promote), these small businesses fail to qualify for loans at most banks. Is it possible to create an environment in which young companies can thrive (and sometimes fail and struggle), create jobs (which they do best), and ultimately blossom into thriving enterprises?

"When politicians criticize government for small-business-strangling regulation, they're being disingenuous," writes Gary Belsky in his Entrepreneurship column for *TIME Business*.[3] "Most small businesses fail to grow because that's the nature of the beast. What you want, from a jobs-creation perspective, is government to foster an environment in which starting a business—period—is easy. It's a numbers game really; since most small businesses will fail or stall, you want to throw as many ideas on the pavement as possible so that the small percentage of startups that thrive is part of an increasing pool of new companies. The success rate may not change, but the absolute number of successes will."

Although I don't think there are any simple answers to the financing needs of Main Street business owners, I think it's time politicians start thinking

---

[2] http://www.nber.org/digest/feb11/w16300.html
[3] http://business.time.com/2012/08/06/start-ups-create-jobs-right-so-why-arent-we-funding-more-small-businesses/

in terms of creating a more "Main Street"–friendly environment so even companies that aren't sexy SaaS[4] startups in Silicon Valley have access to capital.

Belsky suggests that instead of arguing over who is more supportive of small businesses or harping about regulations, maybe it's time politicians on both sides of the aisle "should explain how they'd help wannabe entrepreneurs take the big leap. Because the more of those folks we can guide from fantasy to reality, the more jobs we'll create down the line."

I couldn't have said it better myself.

What Would You Do with an Extra $40,000?

In a paper published by the University of Tennessee's Rob Holland, he cites a Dun & Bradstreet report that claims, "…businesses with fewer than 20 employees have only a 37% chance of surviving four years (in business) and only a 9% chance of surviving 10 years."[5] A lack of funding is part of what causes many small businesses to struggle and ultimately fail.

Several years ago, I started a small business providing digital prepress services to professional portrait photographers. Our little business provided valuable color-correction and retouching services to a number of professional photographers in our market. If we prepared their digital files for printing, they received a discount for printing at one of the local labs.

We had loyal customers and were very busy, but as we started our third year of business, we were having cash flow problems. An extra $8,000 to $10,000 would have made all the difference in the world to us. But I had tapped out my personal savings and credit cards to keep things going and couldn't get a business loan from the bank. Because we weren't a sexy tech startup, equity funding was out of the question.

I eventually had to close shop. Telling my three employees we were done was one of the hardest things I've ever had to do. I've since spoken with many entrepreneurs trying to keep a Main Street business alive who faced the same dilemma. Some survived; some did not.

Although financing woes weren't the only cause of my company's demise, a lack of adequate working capital kills many small businesses, just like mine, every year. We didn't close our doors because we didn't have customers or business—we had more work than we could do with the staff

---

[4]Software as a Service
[5]Rob Holland, "Planning Against a Business Failure," Agricultural Development Center, University of Tennessee

we had. I was often in the office until 1:00 or 2:00 a.m. in those days. I can't count how many times my wife called around midnight to see if I was coming home or to ask if I needed her to bring me a sleeping bag. (The fact that I hadn't taken a regular paycheck during that time made the late hours particularly annoying to the rest of my family.)

Fortunately, there are a lot more options now for small business owners looking for financing.

What's more, don't forget that Main Street business startups all across the country are collectively creating a lot of jobs. My three employees were part of that job-creation statistic. Main Street needs capital to grow and create jobs. The more options for financing they have, the stronger they'll make our communities and the more jobs they'll be able to create.

There Are Other Financing Options

Most small business owners have no other choice but to bootstrap their businesses to get them going. Finding investors for most Main Street businesses carries about the same odds as this 53-year-old beating Olympic Gold Medalist Usain Bolt in the 100-yard dash. It just isn't going to happen.

Like my dad and thousands of other entrepreneurs, I turned to a second mortgage and credit cards to get my business off the ground. Fortunately, many small business owners today have other options to fund working capital or finance growth. Although bankers are still a critical part of small business financing, business owners aren't as dependent on them. Banks are no longer the only place to find the money needed to develop new products and services, grow, and hire people.

Note You have many more options than bank financing to get money to grow, add employees, or launch new initiatives. This book outlines them all.

For many entrepreneurs, the aversion to alternative, unfamiliar funding sources can be more of a handicap than hearing "no" from the bank. The coming chapters cover in detail some of those options. In the meantime, here is a list of just a few of the alternative loan options available to small business owners (even if they have less than perfect credit, haven't been in business for three to five years, and don't have a big bankroll):

- *Accounts receivable (AR)/purchase order (PO) financing*: Many small business owners can leverage their AR or a current PO for short-term working capital loans.

- *Cash advance or merchant cash advance*: Small businesses with regular credit card transactions can borrow against future earnings. Repayment is made by a daily withdrawal from the business merchant account. Repayment terms are typically six months to a year.

- *Commercial real estate loans*: These loans are based upon the value of the real estate offered as collateral and can include office buildings, warehouse space, retail storefronts, industrial facilities, and stand-alone buildings.

- *Equipment financing*: When you finance equipment to be used exclusively for the business, the equipment purchased is considered collateral for the loan. Although equipment financing is used exclusively to acquire business-use equipment, it is sometimes used to obtain cash by borrowing against business equipment you already own.

- *Franchise loans*: Franchise loans are similar to common business and commercial loans, but they are designed to finance the purchase of a franchise that can demonstrate an established history of profitability.

- *Peer-to-peer loans*: Individuals with money to invest for profit participate in P2P lending networks and offer loans to those who may not qualify elsewhere.

- *SBA microloans*: The Small Business Administration Microloan program provides very small loans to new businesses or for small business growth. The lenders are non-profit organizations that offer government funding in specific U.S. counties.

Although some banks and credit unions offer alternative financing options to their customers, a willingness to step outside of the bank or credit union is where small business owners will likely find this type of financing.

Amazon.com and Small Business Financing

A resourceful small business owner can find alternative financing in what just a few short years ago would have been considered unconventional places.

For example, many of the merchants that are part of the Amazon marketplace are small and lack the capital of larger retailers. "Small merchants who generally lack capital to buy the inventory they would like to sell can apply for loans through the service [Amazon Lending]," reports Great Speculations (a team of MIT engineers and Wall Street analysts) via *Forbes*.[6] "The merchant whose application is approved would have the funds transferred to his/her Amazon Seller Account. After that, a monthly payment will be taken out of their account until the loan gets paid off."

As with most non-traditional financing, the interest rate is a little higher than what you might expect from a bank (13%), but then again, it's possible some of these small business owners wouldn't qualify for a bank loan. Amazon Lending approves loans within four days and stipulates that the capital be deployed solely for the Amazon sales channel, but I applaud Amazon for seeing a need among their online venders and coming up with a creative solution to keep the wheels of e-commerce turning.

The Great Speculations group postulates that this could lure sellers from eBay and increase online sales as merchants list more items for sale with increased capital at their disposal. This sounds like a good option for Amazon's merchants and good deal for Amazon.

Although banks and credit unions still provide traditional small business lending, Main Street business owners are finding alternatives (like this program at Amazon) very attractive. The challenge is making the right connection to the lender best suited to the financing needs of the business.

Small Business Isn't for the Faint Hearted

There comes a time in the life of every small business owner when he or she needs more cash for working capital, expansion, or to avert a crisis. Mark Twain supposedly once said, "A banker is a fellow who lends you his umbrella when the sun is shining and wants it back the minute it begins to rain." Although the best time to get a loan is when you don't need one, many of us don't plan that far ahead. If you're reading this book, hopefully that isn't the case for you.

The challenge of keeping customers, employees, and spouses happy (all at the same time) is no small feat. Hopefully you will find the following pages helpful to keep the wheels of your small business turning. The Chinese master Lao Tzu said, "The journey of a thousand miles begins with the first step." Since most small business owners start with a trip to the bank (or credit union), this book starts there too.

---

[6]http://www.forbes.com/sites/greatspeculations/2012/10/05/amazon-wades-into-lending-to-drive-market-place-sales/

Plan of the Book

Building a good working relationship with your banker is critical. I talk about how to get off on the right foot, how to prepare for your visit to the bank, when it's time to pop the question (ask for a loan), and how to make sure you get the right loan for your needs.

Figuring out what loan products are offered by the SBA is no small task either. I talk about what it takes to qualify, where to apply for a loan, and some of the things you can do to improve your chances of getting an SBA loan.

As mentioned, the harsh reality of financing a small business is that only 10% of business owners who make the trip to the bank get a loan. Although leaving the familiar world of the bank waiting room might feel a little like leaving Kansas, I talk about the other options that are available in what might feel like Oz.

No discussion of funding a business venture would be complete without talking about angels, venture capital, and the myth of the shark tank, but I won't stop there. I talk about finding investors, how to evaluate if you're a good fit for VC funding, and what most venture capitalists want in return.

If it doesn't look like you're a fit for *equity funding* (a fancy term for taking money from a venture capitalist and the associated requirement to share equity that goes along with it), you learn how to make an honest evaluation of your situation and where to go from there. I cover a number of non-traditional financing options in detail, including where and how to apply, what to expect, and how to prepare. I also talk about what to do should a crisis arise and you need cash fast.

There are no easy answers to the financing challenges faced by Main Street business owners, but taking that first step is the only way to start.

Building a Relationship with the Bank

Date Before You Marry

Business is personal. I once worked with a guy who didn't think that way, and he worked very hard to avoid having personal relationships with his customers, his employees, and his vendors. That attitude didn't serve him or his business very well, because doing business is a personal endeavor. Just like any worthwhile business relationship, the same holds true for the relationship with your bank. It's important to get to know your banker.

Tip Get to know your banker. You're far more likely to get help when you need it.

Many larger credit unions provide the same types of services that were originally provided only by banks (much to the chagrin of bankers, I might add). Although I refer to banks more often than credit unions in this chapter, most of what applies to one applies to the other. My hope is that neither bankers nor those who offer small business services at a credit union will be offended by my offhanded use of the term "bankers" to describe them both. (However, I know that a couple of my credit union friends might have a thing or two to say about it.)

When my wife and I were first married, we were members of a small credit union that had only a few branches. The branch manager knew and trusted me. Whenever I needed a little extra cash, I could easily borrow a couple thousand dollars against my signature. Even though these types of relationships don't exist much anymore, it doesn't mean that building a good relationship with your banker is any less important.

Over the years, I've seen countless ads from major banks in my area and around the country claiming that, unlike the *other* banks, *their* bank takes their partnership with small businesses seriously. In all honesty, over the years I haven't known too many bankers who treated me as a personal associate, but I've had the chance to work with a *few*.

Getting to Know Your Banker

Several years ago, my partners and I decided to buy a photography supply business. Although it had been around for a while, it was struggling. We thought we could turn things around with a little time, a good dose of marketing, and some elbow grease. Unlike in a traditional camera store, our focus was less on cameras and more on the albums, film, equipment, backdrops, and props a professional photographer uses in the studio every day. We sold cameras, but it wasn't the focus of our business. In many respects it was more of a B2B (business-to-business) enterprise than a traditional camera store.

We had a good local clientele that included the professionals in our area, but we also sold a lot of goods at tradeshows and industry events around the country. At the time, the idea of selling goods online was so new that we had just started to experiment with online sales. Most of our business was generated through the tradeshows and the other events we attended. In fact, there were a couple of guys on our team who spent most of their time on the road every month.

Because our business was so different from a traditional camera store, our relationship with the bank was a little different too. Our banker took the time to learn about our business—in fact, over the years he had become a photography business specialist and worked with a number of the professional photographers in our area. I'm not sure how he stumbled into that particular niche, but he understood what we were doing and over time he became a trusted member of our team. He even made a point of dropping into the store on a regular basis just to say hello and see how we were doing. Like all small business owners, we sometimes had issues with cash flow and needed to increase our line of credit. I don't remember ever going into the bank or jumping through hoops to increase our credit line. He was a real asset to us—and the only banker I've ever known who took the time to get to know our business.

I wish I could tell you there's a secret to getting to know your banker, but there isn't. I *can* tell you that many banks have bankers whose job it is to keep their small business owners happy (some even have special branches that cater to the needs of small businesses). So the first step to building a healthy and productive business relationship with your banker is to visit the branch and introduce yourself. In my experience, you could be waiting a long time if you're waiting for the bank to reach out to you.

With that said, some bankers are taking the relationships they have with their small business clients seriously.

■ **Tip**   Walk into your local bank and introduce yourself. Ask to speak to a lender. Just say hi and tell her about your business and that you may need her help in the near future.

It's All About Relationships

Bob Coleman is a small business banking expert and a frequent guest on Fox Business news. He is oft quoted by *The Wall Street Journal*, Bloomberg, Forbes, CNNMoney, and *The New York Times* regarding small business financing. He also publishes a number of small business loan-underwriting guides in addition to a small business-lending newsletter. In his book, *Money, Money Everywhere But Not a Drop for Main Street*,[1] Coleman suggests:

> *You can imagine how difficult it is for a lender to judge your character when they first eyeball you from across the desk.*

> *The landscape is littered with businesses, Fortune 500 companies, corner coffee shops, and lenders that have gone bankrupt. You have to convince them that you are smarter than companies like General Motors, CIT, Lehman Brothers, and Joe's Coffee Shop.*

There are a lot of smart business owners who, for one reason or another, are part of the group Coleman is talking about. That's why so many bankers focus on credit score, time in business, and annual revenues. Those criteria are important, but your character and experience is becoming more and more important to many bankers. You need to make sure you put your best foot forward in that regard, too.

---

[1]*Money, Money Everywhere But Not a Drop for Main Street* (page 63), Bob Coleman, 2011, Coleman Publishing, www.colemanpublishing.com.

As mentioned earlier, most banks want a credit score of 650 or better, several years in business, and a fat bankroll before they'll talk to you about a loan. However, there are some bankers who are looking for long-term relationships with business owners just like you.

Vicky Beaudry of First Coast Community Bank in Jacksonville, Florida understands what she calls the "new normal" since the financial meltdown. She says:

> I understand that every loan can be structured differently and I'm giving you the perspective of a community bank where we're looking for the deposit relationships, merchant services, and the personal banking needs.
>
> We're trying to know that customer, know their credit, and finally their collateral. But make sure you get character, then collateral.[2]

Beaudry isn't the only banker who takes the time to get to know her customers on a more personal level than their credit score and time in business. When you're shopping around for a loan, I suggest you look for a banker who wants to build that kind of relationship with you. It should be an important factor in choosing a bank.

It makes sense that building a good relationship with your banker requires convincing him that you have good character, that you have a thriving business, and that there is potential for your business to grow. However, the same is true for Mr. or Ms. Banker. It's also up to the banker to convince you that a relationship with them is in your best interest. If they can't do that, they likely shouldn't be your banker.

10 Questions to Ask Your Potential Banker

Some time ago I stumbled upon this great list of questions. Because all banks are not created equal (particularly where small business is concerned), these questions are a good way to determine if you're in the right bank. Mary Goodman and Rich Russakoff, co-founders of Bottom Line Enterprises, originally published the list in *The Money Dept* column for BNET.[3] I have adapted their list and added my own two cents.

---

[2]Bob Coleman, Money, Money Everywhere But Not a Drop for Main Street, Coleman Publishing, www.colemanpublishing.com, 2011. Page 66.
[3]http://www.cbsnews.com/8301-505143_162-48640126/10-questions-to-find-the-right-bank-for-your-business/?tag=mncol;lst;2

- *Is the bank healthy with strong financials?*

  In light of the events of the last few years, I think it goes without saying that this isn't a given, and certainly shouldn't be taken lightly. Regardless of whether they have a fancy lobby and expensive furniture, you should verify the bank's financial health. The FDIC (Federal Deposit Insurance Corporation) doesn't publish a list of troubled banks—imagine the panic if your bank was on the list and you and your fellow customers found out. However, asking the following questions will help you determine whether the bank you're considering is in good financial shape:

  - Have the last 12 months been profitable?

  - Are earnings increasing or decreasing?

  - Are they in the middle of a merger or have they recently been acquired?

  - Do they have adequate liquidity?

  Your banker should be willing and able to answer these questions to your satisfaction *before* you establish a relationship with him. If he can't or won't give you a straight answer, you should probably look for another bank *and* another banker.

  Even when you have a long-standing relationship with your current bank, don't take that relationship for granted. Even some established banks are struggling these days. What's more, the things they let small business owners get away with just a few short years ago (such as floating an overdrawn account for a couple of days), they don't anymore. Recent economic times have forced bankers to be more dogmatic in how they enforce the policies listed in the fine print.

■ **Tip** Consider it a red flag when the loan officer won't discuss the bank's financial health. Look elsewhere for a long-term relationship.

- *Does the bank have a business division focused on lending to small- and medium-sized companies?*

  Don't take for granted that they do. Even more important might be determining the percentage of small business customers they have. One of the easiest ways to do this is to determine if they have a small business-specific listing in the phone book or on their website. The banker you're interviewing (yes, treat this the same way you would any interview with a potential employee or partner) might have a brochure or other literature that highlights their business banking services.

  Most banks are very "old school" when it comes to their marketing and advertising. In other words, their billboards and the type of events they sponsor tell you a lot about the banking customers they are looking for. Driving into work every day, I see several billboards for different banks and credit unions advertising for small business banking customers. I know it's not very high tech, but it can be a great way to start looking. (I offer more suggestions on where to find a list of potential banks later in this chapter.)

  In my area, a certain bank has been recognized as the small business loan leader for several years. In the months before those statistics come out, they always push for SBA (Small Business Administration) loans. The number two small business lender in the area is one of the bigger credit unions. I've often wondered why the bank spends so much time and money in the month or two leading up to the ranking trying to convince small business owners to borrow at their bank, and the credit union doesn't. Maybe number two is doing a better job of consistently providing great business services and small business lending throughout the year. If I were looking for a new banking relationship in this market, I might check out number two.

  If you can't find the information you're looking for anywhere else, it never hurts to ask the banker whether small business banking is one of their specialties.

- *Is the bank on the SBA's current list of top small business lenders?*

  Information on the top SBA lenders in the country is available from the Small Business Administration,[4] which also provides a downloadable PDF of the top lenders in every state.[5] Goodman and Russakoff also recommend *Entrepreneur* magazine's list of the Best Banks for Entrepreneurs.[6]

- *Is the bank familiar with your industry?*

  Although you might think that one small business relationship or loan is the same as any other, they are different. My partners and I enjoyed the benefits of a banking partner who understood our business. Because every industry is a little bit different, some banks and bankers focus on particular types of small businesses. When looking for a loan or other financial services, it's not unreasonable to expect the banker or loan officer to be able to answer your industry-specific banking questions, as well as tell you how she will provide better services to your business than another financial institution. If she can't do this, ask for a recommendation of a bank or credit union in your area that knows your industry. (Most local bankers have a pretty good handle on their competitors and are usually willing to help you find a match.) In very small markets, the local bank might have to be a jack-of-all-trades. In this case, you may need to look outside your local market to find the right bank. I know several software companies local to my area, for example, with banking relationships in Silicon Valley because they feel that a Bay Area bank better understands their industry. Don't be afraid to bank out of town if that best suits your needs.

---

[4]http://www.sba.gov/category/lender-navigation/lender-loan-data/100-most-active-sba-7a-lenders
[5]www.sba.gov/sites/default/files/sbl_11study%20FINAL.pdf
[6]http://www.entrepreneur.com/bestbanks

- *Does the bank offer the mix of services and products you want?*

  Depending on the business you're in, you'll likely want merchant services, a checking account, and maybe even a business credit card. But don't stop there. You may also want a line of credit or access to capital via a real estate loan or equipment financing. Depending on the type of business and the industry you're in, some banking services are more important than others. Don't be afraid to ask about the services you *think* you'll need *before* you need them. Finding out too late that your bank doesn't offer the particular services you need can handicap your success.

- *Does your desired loan amount fit within the bank's lending limits?*

  I'm going to assume, since you are reading this book, that one of your primary objectives is to learn how to best obtain financing for working capital or funding growth. It's reasonable and smart to ask your potential banker about the average loan size his bank offers small businesses. This is even more important when you consider what your future needs might be as your business grows. Will this bank be able to grow with you as your needs increase?

  Some smaller banks have ceilings on how much they can loan any one business. I know a business owner who had great credit, had been with the same bank for several years, and had successfully paid off several small loans over the course of doing business with that bank, but couldn't get financing because the new loan would exceed the ceiling his bank lends any single business. He had to look elsewhere for financing and ultimately ended up going through the pain of finding a new banker because his current bank wasn't big enough to accommodate his needs.

- *Is the decision-maker someone you can meet with?*

  When the time comes to secure a loan, will you be able to meet with the bank officers who ultimately make the lending decisions? Of course, this is no guarantee that you'll get the loan, but it doesn't hurt to know the bank president or other senior executives who can vouch for you and your relationship with the bank. As mentioned earlier, most banks are more interested in your credit score, years in business, and your account balance, but there are bankers like Ms. Beaudry who consider reputation and character just as important as credit score. (This is particularly true with smaller banks, where the bank president makes it a point to know all of her small business customers.)

- *Is the banker willing to meet with you at your company?*

  I would have never known this was a big deal until I had a banker who regularly met with us at our place of business. If the only thing your banker does to understand your business is look at your balance sheet, he is getting only a part of the picture. For example, if your business presents well (in other words, it looks good to outsiders or visitors), it's a good idea to have your banker visit the office. There's something about seeing your customers, or the volume of merchandise you ship, that makes a difference in how you're perceived. There's nothing wrong with trying to conduct business with your banker on *your* turf. Doing business at the bank is a lot like getting bad news and advice about your health from your doctor when you're in your underwear, with a flimsy gown on, vulnerable, and uninformed about what's going on. Your banker, like the doctor, has more of the control and authority when you're sitting across his desk inside a nicely furnished bank office.

  Speaking from experience, I know that the banker I've previously mentioned felt more invested in the success and health of our business because he was often there when customers were in the store. He saw firsthand that we had a loyal customer base and a thriving business—which made it a lot easier to get help when we needed it. What's more, I don't remember even going into his office in those days—we always conducted business in our store.

▓ **Note**   If your banker visits your place of business on a regular basis, consider yourself lucky and treasure that person.

- *Are loan decisions made locally?*

  If the ultimate decision about your small business loan application goes to a loan approval board that may or may not be in the same city (or even the same state for that matter), the only information they'll have to make a decision about your loan is your balance sheet and how well you look to them on paper (credit score, time in business, and account history). Even some homegrown banks don't give lending authority to their individual branches. In fact, the credit union I've been a member of for years no longer allows individual branch managers to make those decisions, as they did in years past. However, some of the largest national and international banks still leave lending decisions to each branch. Don't assume because the bank is local that they will have local lending authority or that the national bank won't. Ask.

- *How long has the loan officer been with the bank?*

  Regardless of how old she may be, I advise you to work with someone who has experience as they help you with your small business loan. It's important that she has the experience she needs not only to help you through the paper work, but also to add value to the process. I understand that everyone has to learn at some point—they just don't have to learn at your expense. If your loan officer seems to be fumbling around and unsure of what she should do, it's not unreasonable to ask if there's someone with more experience who can help you.

Which Local Bank Is Courting Small Businesses?

As mentioned earlier, some banks are more interested in courting small businesses than others. Or, rather, some banks will be more interested in doing business with you than others. The trick is determining which banks they are. As promised, here are a few more suggestions to finding the right bank. Russakoff and Goodman[7] suggest a few places where you might

---

[7]http://www.cbsnews.com/8301-505143_162-48640118/what-you-need-to-know-if-youre-trying-to-get-a-bank-loan/?tag=bnetdomain

find banks that are courting small businesses. Treat your search for a bank much like a prospecting exercise. Start with a list, do your homework, and prepare to ascertain the information noted previously. Then narrow down your list to a few banks that look like a good fit, and interview them all before you make a decision. I call this the "Beauty Pageant method" and, much like the Miss America Pageant, the interview carries a lot of points. Here are some ways to build your list:

- Talk to your business peers (Russakoff and Goodman suggest this might be the best place to look, and I agree)

- Ask your biggest customers where they bank

- Ask your suppliers, vendors, and other professional service providers where they bank

- Contact applicable trade associations

- Scour online resources such as ibank,[8] sba.gov,[9] LinkedIn,[10] Lendio,[11] or whatever pops up during a simple Google[12] search

Never Forget: Banking Is a Business

While you're standing in the lobby waiting for someone to help you, it's easy to forget that banking is a business and you are a potential customer. I've met with bankers who tried to make me feel like I was fortunate they were even talking to me. The truth is, regardless of how big the bank is or how small your business is, one of the biggest challenges facing many bankers every day is finding new customers.

As mentioned earlier, most bank marketing is old school. When looking for new business, many bankers rely on a referral network of CPAs, the Chamber of Commerce, insurance agents, and traditional marketing like billboards, radio, and the events they sponsor. When you go into the bank to open an account or to apply for a loan, they are looking for good customers every bit as much as you want to be one.

---

[8] http://www.ibank.com/
[9] http://www.sbaonline.sba.gov/
[10] http://www.linkedin.com/
[11] http://www.lendio.com/
[12] http://www.google.com

Remember, even though you are going to be the bank's customer, you need to make sure you put your best foot forward. I don't think that means you need to wear a suit and tie or your Sunday best, but you do need to look professional, have your financial records in order, and be ready to make them salivate to do business with you.

Summary

Despite how it might feel when a banker or two turns down your loan request, finding someone you can build a good working relationship with isn't a pipe dream. In fact, it can make the difference down the road. The next chapter discusses how the banker looks at you when you first sit down across the desk and talk about your financing needs.

Keeping Your Relationship Personal

When the Honeymoon Is Over

Once upon a time there was a very motivated banker. He was my banker. I mentioned him earlier.

My partners and I had a great relationship with our bank and that banker. His unique understanding of what we were doing made him a very valuable asset to us.

He went out of his way to make sure we were taken care of. In fact, other than making deposits at the drive-through, I don't think we ever did any business inside the bank—he would visit us at our store. I had his personal cell number and could call him anytime I had questions. Our relationship with this banker worked, because *he* worked for *us*.

Unfortunately, not all bankers are like this and in most cities around the country, this isn't what banks really want their loan officers doing anyway (at least that's how it feels). Nevertheless, I still believe a personal relationship with your banker is important. When we were starting out, our relationship with the banker often determined whether we got the financing we needed. Although that might not be true anymore, a good banker can still help you navigate some of the myriad options available (even if he or she can't determine whether you get a loan). Remember, in big national banks and regional banks, a loan committee usually makes those decisions.

It's likely no surprise to anyone reading this book that, following the financial meltdown of 2008, securing the financing needed for working capital and fueling growth has been difficult for small business owners. This clampdown on the local bank's ability or willingness to lend money to Main Street hurt a lot of small business owners. However, it's also created an opportunity for alternative lenders who have stepped in and offered sometimes unique options to businesses looking for alternatives (which you learn about in detail in subsequent chapters).

It also has some bankers thinking about how to keep their best customers in *their* bank.

In my opinion, this is good for small business owners. I don't know if the percentage of small business owners who apply for a loan at the local bank will increase anytime soon, but I believe anything that gets bankers out from behind their collective desks and into the offices of their customers, to help *them* be successful, is a good thing.

Like any other vendor, small business owners need to start looking at their bankers as strategic partners. As easy as it might be to blame the lack of relationship on the bank, there are some things a Main Street business owner can do to build a more personal relationship with his or her banker.

▓ **Tip**   Look at your bankers as strategic partners. Invite them in to view your business first hand; ask their advice when you need help. They see a lot of businesses, successful and otherwise. An insightful banker is valuable to your business.

Five Ways to Maintain a Great Relationship with Your Banker

Like any good relationship, a personal working relationship with your banker doesn't just happen. It all comes down to communication.

- *Personally communicate with your banker at least once every quarter:* This is a great time to share positive company news. You might also want to add her e-mail address to your mailing list. That way, when press announcements are made or when you make a new product announcement, she will hear about it.

Over time, your banker will get accustomed to hearing from you and will appreciate your willingness to treat her like a partner. Most people don't like to be the person who gets a call only when somebody wants something—neither does your banker.

- *Invite your banker over to "your" turf*: A couple of years ago, Kraft's Dana Anderson spoke at a Forrester Marketing event about the importance of creating an effective environment to foster cross-departmental collaboration. One of the major takeaways was the idea of inviting collaboration partners to spend time on your turf and sharing with them what you're doing. Sharing your success, she said, is crucial to initiatives that require cross-departmental buy-in. I believe this is relevant to building a personal relationship with your banker. I think meeting us on our turf gave our banker a better understanding of what we were doing at the photography supply business. He watched us answer the phones and talk to customers. He witnessed first-hand the positive relationship we had with our photographers. He saw what we were doing and had a greater understanding when we needed to increase our business credit line for a special situation.

- *Don't forget holidays and birthdays*: Set yourself apart from all the other small business clients by remembering your banker's birthday, or holidays, with a personalized greeting card. If for no other reason than nobody else is doing it, take advantage of the opportunity to stay top-of-mind with your banker. You're likely sending greeting cards to customers already; one more card to your banker is a very small investment.

- *Don't fudge the numbers*: Even if you have a good relationship with your banker, you have to make sure the numbers jibe. Even a small mistake on your P&L could wreak havoc down the road if your financial information isn't accurate. Your banker will be less likely to help you find the loan you need if your financial information is traditionally filled with mistakes. Nobody wants to make excuses for what might be considered sloppiness on your part.

- *Don't make your banker the last to know:* When you have bad news, don't let your banker find out through the grapevine. Make sure your banker hears your side of the story before he reads about it in the news or hears about it from someone else. Years ago, one of my dad's suppliers was distributing faulty products to their network of distributors. The negative press and the subsequent fallout impacted a number of businesses within their distribution network, including my father's business. When his banker read about it in the news—and perhaps because he didn't hear anything from my dad—he assumed the worst and called a loan due immediately. This was a tough blow for the business to be sure. I can't help but wonder if the situation would have been different if the banker hadn't been the last to know. He didn't have a chance to hear my dad's story or his contingency plans. The banker had no other information upon which to base a decision than the news reports.

Don't forget that your banker is your banker. Although you want a personal and cordial relationship, it might not be a good idea to become an "open book." He or she is part of the decision-making team at your bank, not your best friend, your therapist, or your clergy. Don't air your dirty laundry at the bank. Be selective about any *relevant* bad news you share; and never whine, moan, or complain about your business or the negative effects of the economy to your banker.

Note   Remember that your banker is . . . your banker. Your banker is not your shrink or your bar buddy. Keep it professional.

You Better Shop Around

As a young man growing up in the 1970s, I'm almost embarrassed to admit that I occasionally listened to the Captain and Tennille. For some reason, thinking about finding the right bank reminds me of their tune, "You Better Shop Around." (Although The Miracles recorded the same tune in the 1950s, the version I'm most familiar with is the former.)

That song offers good advice when it comes time to find a lender. The local bank is likely the best place to start, but don't let your search end there.

It goes without saying that you'll need some kind of checking account, maybe even a credit card or line of credit, but there's a lot more to finding the right bank (and banker for that matter). Although most banks look the same on the outside, and maybe even on the inside, some focus on different things. You may even find bankers who specialize in one type of business over another.

Many high-tech companies where I live (Utah) choose to use a Silicon Valley-based bank. They feel the banks in the Bay Area are better equipped and more experienced working with tech firms than the local banks. I'm not suggesting you do that, but you could. Technology makes it possible for you to do your banking almost anywhere in the country—much to the chagrin of the local bank. You're not married or limited to the services they offer "around the corner."

With that said, in most markets you have options—even if you choose to bank locally. In fact, many credit unions offer small business banking services. Additionally, the biggest bank in your market might not be the best for you. You better shop around.

Good Relationships Start with Good Choices

Before you begin, make sure you have a good idea what you're looking for. Does your Main Street business have specialized financing needs or are you looking for a banker who can give you investment advice? If you have highly specialized needs, jumping online might be the best place to start. You can search for local (or not so local) banks that specialize in what you're looking for.

Some banks offer incentives for maintaining an average daily balance above a certain threshold. Will large amounts of cash be flowing through your account? Are there fees or penalties for large numbers of transactions? If you don't already have a cash flow–management plan, it's a good idea to have one *before* you start comparing banks. Some banks even offer those services and can offer information about your specific industry.

My first small business banking relationship was a business checking account. I didn't give much thought to the other services I might need in the future, and it caused me grief down the road. Look down the road five or ten years to identify the services you may need over time.

Tip Think of where you want your business to be in 5 or 10 years. Make sure you pick a bank that will be able to service your needs at that point in the life of your business.

Apples and Oranges in Banking

If all you're looking for are basic services like a checking account, you might even look into online banking. Many brick-and-mortar banks offer online services that are accessible wherever you are. I'm amazed at the number of simple banking services I can access via my smart phone.

Nevertheless, if you see the need for financing to fund working capital, purchase equipment, or other similar needs, a face-to-face relationship with a live banker offers value you can't find if you do all your banking online or by phone. Additionally, if easy access to deposits and cash is important to you, multiple branches and an extensive ATM network could be what you're looking for.

Don't forget, at most banks, the services you use often come with associated fees. For example, the fees small businesses pay are often different (and usually higher) than those associated with a personal checking account. Sometimes there are fees associated with the number of transactions you process or whether you use online banking services. Don't be shy to ask about any associated fees. They add up. If you're looking for free banking services, make sure you talk about it before you make a commitment. After all, the bank is there to serve your needs, not the other way around.

In a Relationship, Does Size Matter?

I mentioned this conversation earlier, but it's worth repeating. I recently had a conversation with a small business owner who unsuccessfully went to the bank he'd been a faithful customer at for many years. He had a reputation as a good customer and had even taken and successfully paid off a number of small business loans during his lifetime as a customer. He had plenty of cash in the bank, his business was healthy, and he had a wonderful credit rating—but he couldn't get the loan he needed to fund a very exciting expansion opportunity.

When he discussed this with his banker, with whom he had a great relationship, he was told that the loan he wanted would make him too big a customer for their community bank. Basically, they couldn't put so many of *their* eggs into *his* basket.

Does size matter? Yes.

He needed an alternative funding source to finance his immediate needs for expansion while he began the search for a new, and bigger, bank.

That doesn't mean a bigger bank with a national footprint is the right bank for you. In the post-credit crisis, many Main Street businesses have turned to smaller banks because they are traditionally more likely to offer financing to local businesses. You might be interested to know that although small and midsize banks are only 22% of the market, in 2009 they accounted for 54% of small business lending according to the Federal Deposit Insurance Company[1] and the Institute for Local Self-Reliance.

Note   Smaller banks occupy 22% of the market, but make 54% of the loans to small business. In many cases, the big guys just won't care about you as much.

What's more, you're likely to garner a little more attention from the community bank down the street than from a national bank. After all, part of the charter that governs a community bank's mission is to help the local neighborhoods thrive. If you want a personal relationship with your banker, a community bank could be the place to look. You should know, however, that the bank and banker I described in the first part of this chapter was a very large bank with a national footprint. We just happened to get a very good banker, and the same thing could happen to you with a large bank.

Do You Need to Redefine the Relationship?

As time goes on and your business grows, changes, and expands, it's a good idea to test the waters periodically and see if there's an opportunity to do better. Just like the small business owner I described earlier, you may discover that you've outgrown your current bank.

You may be surprised to find, as a more established business, you have a lot more clout when it comes to negotiating interest rates or eliminating bank service fees. That's because you'll be viewed as a less risky bet. If you're meeting with your banker every quarter as suggested, you'll have plenty of time to discuss your changing business needs, your track record as a customer, and what you expect from your banker and the bank. This is a great time to discuss any additional services you might need and whether your current bank will be able to provide them.

You may also decide that you need different accounts with different banks for different reasons. For example, it's not uncommon for a small business to have a separate payroll account at a different bank. Many banks maintain a separate merchant account for processing credit card transactions.

---

[1] http://www.ilsr.org/charts-small-banks-small-business-lending/

Managing my credit card transactions felt like one of the most complicated and cumbersome banking experiences I ever had to deal with, so I liked keeping my merchant transactions in a separate account.

Your Best Interests at Heart

It might be easy to assume that a banker who agrees with you and always gives you what you want has your best interests at heart, but that might not be the case. I've tried to tell my wife that capitulating to my every whim is a good idea for over 30 years, but I have yet to convince her. In fact, she often gives me news I don't like and opinions that are contrary to mine. Some of those traits might be worthwhile in a banker too—here are three of them:

- *She encourages me to interact with others*: I'm not in the least bit anti-social, but my sweet wife sometimes thinks the time I spend on my motorcycle alone is excessive (although I consider it valuable battery-recharging time). She encourages me to spend more time socializing with our friends and adult children. This is sometimes problematic, since few of them ride motorcycles. In the same vein, a banker with your best interests at heart will make sure you have an opportunity to meet and network with people who can help your business. Bankers know a lot of people. People you likely *don't* know. Hopefully your banker is invested in your success and is always looking for ways to provide value to you and your business. Sometimes that means helping you make connections with people who can help you meet your financial objectives. This is a potential win/win situation for everyone, provided you're willing to let them broaden your circle of influence.

- *My wife wants me to be successful*: We've been married for a long time and she feels the impact of my success on a daily basis. A banker who has your best interests at heart wants you to be successful in the same way. Lest you think that requires bankers to be totally altruistic, your success bodes well for them too. The more successful you are, the more likely your banker will be able to provide the services you need and generate revenue for the bank. You should expect the financial strategies your banker recommends to be mutually beneficial—and that is a good thing.

- *My wife tells me the truth:* She might not always tell me what I want to hear, but I can always trust that she is telling me what she thinks I need to hear. Honest feedback is often difficult to accept. If your banker really has your best interests at heart, he will give you honest feedback. Of course, he'll share your optimism for the future, but there may be times when he also shares frank and honest concerns about what he sees as risks. Your banker may even uncover potential problems that he can help you solve.

It's doubtful that you'll ever feel like your banker is your BFF—she is your banker after all. However, it's not unreasonable to expect she will treat your relationship the same way you treat it—as an investment.

Keeping the Honeymoon Alive

There are as many suggestions for nurturing a good banking relationship as there are bankers. Mitch Hurley, formerly a Vice President at First Security Bank of Utah, used to call them the three Ts:

- *Talk:* Communication is critical for any relationship to thrive. Have you ever had a spouse or close friend say something like, "Talk to me." I'm ashamed to admit if I've been "focused" on work or some other distraction, I sometimes need to be reminded that communication is important. The same is true regarding your relationship with your banker. The conversations need to be frank and regular.

- *Time:* Nothing happens overnight. It took a while for my wife to realize that I was awesome, just like it might take you and your banker time to build a strong relationship. Don't force things and don't assume that simply because you're a customer at the bank, the banker is going to love you instantly. Don't rush things. Take your time.

- *Trust:* Honest Communication + Time = Trust. Trust is the foundation of any worthwhile relationship. I suggest you spend the same time and energy with your banker that you spend creating these types of relationships with your vendors and customers.

▓ **Note** Trust isn't born overnight. It takes a combination of honesty and time to develop trust. Establishing this kind of trust puts you in a position of strength when you visit the bank.

Improve Your Odds of Success

Having a good working relationship with your banker is all fine and good, but if we're honest, the reason we do it is to improve our odds at those times when we need capital to cover a cash-flow issue, fuel expansion, or to help a customer with a special project. Bankers are typically very conservative. Relationship building is about giving your banker as many reasons to have confidence in you as possible.

Bankers are risk averse (derivatives scandals aside). A good relationship with your banker combined with an understanding of how credit works will help you in the long run. Here are a couple of suggestions that will help you maintain a good relationship with the bank and relate in terms you banker understands:

- *Avoid surprises:* Don't wait until the last minute to let your banker know you need a loan. If you have a good relationship with your banker and are communicating with him regularly, there should be no reason to make the panicked, "I need a loan tonight or I'm going to have to close my doors" phone call. If you have a good relationship, your banker will want to help you, but he also has a responsibility to protect depositor assets. It's amazing how much easier this process is if you are regularly communicating with your banker, he regularly visits you on your turf, and he understands what you do and why your request for a loan is a good idea.

- *Don't limit yourself to just one bank (or banker):* Although this might sound counterintuitive (and your banker will likely not admit it), this spreads the risk around, making you a safer investment. Like every other working relationship, bankers move around, change roles, and get promoted. It's a good idea to foster good relationships with more than one banker at your primary bank. If you nurture positive relationships with more than one banker at more than one bank, you'll have more options when you're in a pinch.

Don't expect your banker to make the first move, but most will appreciate your efforts to initiate a good working relationship. It might sound one-sided, but if your banker trusts your character, knows you are credible, and you've spent the time to build a good working relationship, you might find yourself one of the 10% of customers who walks out of the bank with a loan.

Summary

Although most small business owners today don't have the same kind of relationships that owners had with their bankers 50 years ago, I believe that developing that relationship is still important. Despite the fact that many banks *and* bankers spend more time evaluating your bottom line, there are those like Dana Anderson who speak out about how important relationship building is for bankers and their small business customers. The next chapter talks about getting the right bank loan.

Getting the Right Bank Loan

My Porridge Is Too Hot!

As a little boy, I loved the story called *The Three Bears*, but it also frustrated me. I didn't think Goldilocks was that bright. Who would eat the porridge, break the chair, and then crash in the bed upstairs? Nevertheless, the story teaches us that one size does not fit all—a lesson that is particularly relevant to small business financing.

When looking for a loan at the bank, you'll likely hear about term loans and lines of credit. It's important to determine which option is "just right" for you and your situation.

Term Loans

This is probably the type of loan most Main Street business owners think of when they head to the bank looking for a loan. In its simplest terms, a term loan is repaid in regular payments over a period of time. Auto loans and home mortgages are both great examples. Amounts and repayment terms vary depending upon the amount borrowed and the credit worthiness of the borrower, but both loan types are term loans.

CREDIT WORTHINESS AND PERSONAL GUARANTEES

As a small business owner, it's important that you pay attention to your personal credit as well as your business credit. For example, if you're the sole proprietor, your personal credit and your business credit are closely linked in the eyes of your bank. However, many Main Street business owners rely too heavily on their personal credit to run their businesses. This can put your personal assets at risk should you find your business in trouble.

When you're starting out, or if your business is very young, your banker might ask for a personal guarantee (in fact, you should expect it). Basically, you're telling your banker that you will be personally liable should your business default on your loan.

I recently heard from a small business borrower who fell behind on a substantial loan and is now facing foreclosure. The commercial property that was used as collateral has been substantially devalued over the last few years and will likely cover only 50–60% of the loan amount. His personal *guarantee* put his personal *assets* at risk, and his attorney is telling him that he will likely lose everything.

It's Usually Buried in the Small Print

They call it "mouse type" in the biz. It's the itty-bitty type at the bottom or backside of the page that only a mouse can read. It outlines all the terms and conditions associated with a term loan. This is true for any loan not just term loans, and it's a good idea to read it and make sure you understand it. Unfortunately, it's usually filled with a lot of legal jargon and the size of the type is actually designed to make it difficult to read. But regardless of your desire to gloss over it, ignoring the fine print can cost you a lot of money and heartache down the road.

Two questions you'll want to answer in the fine print are:

Is your interest rate fixed or floating? A fixed rate of interest means the percentage of interest will never change over the term of your loan, regardless of the financial markets. A good time to take out a fixed rate loan is when interest rates are low. Floating interest rates fluctuate with the market. When interest rates are generally low, you will enjoy a lower interest rate on your business loan. When rates go up, so will the interest rate on your loan. So having an adjustable rate loan could be good or bad depending upon what happens with the economy.

Is it simple or compounding interest? It's amazing how such simple concepts can be so confusing and expensive if you don't fully understand them. In a nutshell, simple interest is calculated only on the principal amount.

In other words, interest is computed on the amount of the loan that remains unpaid at any given time. The formula looks like this:

Principal (Loan) Amount x Interest Rate x Time in Years = Simple
Interest
(Total)

For example, imagine you have a $1,000 loan for equipment. The interest rate is 5% per annum and the loan is to be repaid in 24 months. That formula looks like this:

$$\$1,000 \times .05 \times 2 = \$100$$

Why 2 instead of 24? Because the interest rate is an annual rate of 5%, so you need to turn the payment terms into years as well.

Compounding interest, on the other hand, requires the borrower not only to pay on the principal amount, but it includes any outstanding interest at any given point in time. Consider the same scenario to understand the difference:

Simple Interest

Year 1: $1,000 x 1 year x 5% = $50 in interest

Year 2: $1,000 x 1 year x 5% = $50 in interest

Total amount of interest paid: $100

Total of principal and interest: $1,100

Compounding Interest

Year 1: $1,000 x 1 year x 5% = $50 in interest

Year 2: $1,050 x 1 year x 5% = $52.50 in interest

Total amount of interest paid: $102.50

Total of principal and interest: $1,102.50

Although this is a very simple example, notice that in year two of the compounding interest, you must pay interest on your principal as well as on the outstanding $50 in interest due. It is expected that regular payments will be made over the course of the loan; the calculations would reflect a monthly payment schedule rather than a yearly payment schedule. Typically, in the beginning, most of the payment is applied toward paying the interest, with a smaller percentage going toward the principal. As the loan matures over time, this ratio changes and more of the principal is paid off with each payment.

As you might guess, if you anticipate paying off your loan early, a simple interest loan is better. Principal and interest are paid off at the same rate. Because a compounding interest loan is weighted with more interest at the front end of the loan, it may feel as if you are being penalized for prepayment.

▧ **Note** Although it might make sense—and can even look good on your credit report—to pay off a loan early, the bank wants your interest payments, and truth be told doesn't want you to pay off your loan early.

Hopefully you can see that the type of interest you pay is every bit as important as the interest rate. It's natural to ask about the interest rate, but just make sure you also ask about the type of interest you'll be paying. It might not feel like it, but don't forget, you are the bank's customer. If your banker is unwilling to go through this information with you, there are other fish in the sea. Maybe it's time for a new banker.

Could a Term Loan be *Just Right* for You and Your Business?

Goldilocks taught us that one size does not fit all, which is why a term loan might not be the right fit for your business. That being said, there are some great advantages to term loans:

- *Immediate access:* Most people are familiar with an auto loan or home mortgage. The entire loan amount is immediately available to purchase equipment, fund working capital, fuel growth, and so on.

- *It's like clockwork:* Budgeting is a piece of cake. You can anticipate your payment and make sure your business allocates funds every month to pay the monthly obligation. There are seldom surprises.

- *Nothing is arbitrary:* Your bank will charge you the agreed-upon rate. There are no arbitrary-feeling interest rate hikes regardless of what's happening in financial markets.

- *The books are easy:* Accounting entries for loan payments are straightforward and easy to reconcile. This isn't an accounting nightmare.

- *Slow and steady wins the race:* This is a great way to establish or improve your company's business credit. Making regular payments over time demonstrates your credit-worthiness to the bank for subsequent (and potentially greater) access to financing.

Despite some of the advantages of a term loan, it isn't all peaches and cream. There are some disadvantages too:

- *Change is hard:* If you get in a bind, or for any reason need to change the terms of your loan, you will need to go through the process of applying and qualifying for a new loan. Waiting until you're in dire straits to go through this process is *not* a good idea. If you have a good relationship with your banker, he may have ideas as to how to approach the bank *before* things go completely south (see previous chapter).

- *You could be left holding the bag:* If interest rates go down, you could be paying a higher-than-market interest rate for your loan. Make sure you can live with the interest rate and are willing to either bite your tongue or find another loan should rates drop.

- *Another loan might not be an option:* Even if you're prepared to find another loan, some loans include prepayment penalties that make jumping ship for a lower interest rate problematic.

Tip Use any loan opportunity as a way to show your banker you are reliable. Paying off your loan on time and without hiccups makes getting the next one easier.

A Line of Credit

Although most people are looking for a term loan, a line of credit probably comes in a close second. Unlike a term loan, a line of credit is a source of funds that you can draw against when the need arises. Additionally, interest is paid only on the amount of funds used. For example, if you have a $10,000 line of credit but access only $5,000 to purchase a new piece of equipment, you pay interest and make payments only on the $5,000 you used.

Although it's not exactly the same, this type of financial instrument is not that different from how trade was conducted in the early days of banking when Italian, Dutch, and English bankers offered a line of credit to international traders buying and selling goods throughout the world. You might also be interested to know that this type of financing was once the most common currency in international trade finance.

Today, a line of credit comes in many different forms. The most relatable is your bank overdraft protection. I don't think most people think of it as a line of credit, but fundamentally, when you overdraw your personal checking account and the bank covers the amount, they do it with a loan. It's likely you have a fixed amount over which your bank or credit union won't honor your checks. It might be $800, $1,000, or more. In reality, that's a line of credit associated with your checking account.

Most of the time, a line of credit is accessed at the borrower's discretion, but not always. The overdraft credit line described previously is a good example of your line of credit being accessed for you.[1]

The term "line of credit" is also used to describe the amount of money the bank is willing to loan you at any given time. If I were to walk into my bank seeking a personal loan, my banker would look at the outstanding balance (if any) on my credit cards, overdraft protection, and auto loan to determine whether I've exceeded my "line of credit." However, generally speaking, a line of credit is a predetermined amount of funds available for access as needed.

In a previous chapter, you learned about a small business owner I knew who was denied a loan by his local bank because it would have exceeded the limit they could loan to any one bank customer. In the simplest terms, that particular loan would have exceeded his "line of credit."

Secured or Unsecured, That Is the Question

Not all lines of credit are created equal. Depending on the type of credit line, your credit history, and your relationship with your bank, you might not need to secure your line of credit with collateral. I mentioned previously that early in my career, I regularly accessed $1,000 to $2,000 when needed on my signature. Although it wasn't a formal line of credit as defined today, those amounts fell within the line of credit the bank was willing to lend me and my business without any collateral (other than my signature).

---

[1] I suppose you could argue that overdrawing your account is accessing your line of credit, but I don't think many people think of it that way.

A home equity credit line is a great example of a secured line of credit. Basically, it is a second mortgage that is available on demand for home improvements. The same type of credit line exists for small businesses.

Some banks will consider a CD or other savings vehicle as security (read "collateral") for a line of credit, but real estate, equipment, accounts receivable, or the company's operating business assets are more commonly used as collateral.

Unlike an unsecured line of credit, a secured line of credit often provides access to a greater amount of cash at a lower interest rate. Credit limits can sometimes be as much as 10 times higher when you're seeking a secured line of credit. Don't forget, your banker wants to minimize risk. When you put "skin in the game" with collateral, that loan is less risky.

■ **Note**   A secured line of credit will give you better rates and access to a larger amount of cash. But never forget that your assets are on the line.

Is a Line of Credit *Just Right* for You and Your Business?

Like a term loan, there are advantages and disadvantages associated with a line of credit. Some of the advantages include:

- *It's There When You Need It:* Unlike a term loan, a line of credit is there when you need it, and it doesn't cost you interest when you don't. Many businesses use their credit line to manage the ups and downs of cash flow.

- *"I'm not worthy":* A line of credit is a good way to demonstrate your credit-worthiness for potentially larger cash needs down the road. Using your credit line builds a positive credit history as you access the credit when you need it and make regular payments to repay it.

- *You gotta be flexible:* Most business credit lines have variable interest rates that fluctuate with the rise and fall of the financial markets. In reality, this is a double-edged sword. You may have inexpensive access to capital when rates are low, but it can feel like a millstone is tied around your neck when rates go up.

- *It's simple:* Many banks offer simple interest on business credit lines, so it's always good to ask upfront if this is the case.

There are also disadvantages:

- *A loan by any other name is still a loan:* Although a line of credit can be used to soften the pain of short-term cash-flow needs, don't forget that it's still a loan. It's a debt that has to be paid. Far too many overly optimistic small business owners tap out their line of credit month after month during tough times because they think happier days are just around the corner. When times are tough, making regular payments on your credit line can become a real burden. I speak from experience here. At best, a line of credit can sometimes do nothing more than put off the inevitable when times are tough, but it can also pound a few additional nails in the coffin if used unwisely.

- *Interest might not be the only expense:* It's not uncommon for some banks to charge up-front fees to establish the line. Most of us don't pay a lot of attention to the fees we are charged—a little here for credit card processing and a little there for check handling. Unnoticed fees add up. Don't forget the mouse type here. Make sure you understand any fees and are prepared to pay them.

- *Should the worst happen:* Your business is liable for any unpaid credit line, the same as any other loan should your business flounder and fail. What's more, if your line of credit is secured with some form of collateral, it's at risk and the bank will likely take it. Additionally, if your bank required a personal guarantee, the bank will come after your personal assets.

Tip Don't ignore the fees associated with your loan. Little costs add up over time. You might be able to find a better deal at the bank around the corner.

When Is the Timing *Just Right?*

Once I decided she was the girl for me, I wanted to make sure the timing was right before I got down on one knee and proposed to my future wife. More importantly, I wanted to make sure I knew what the answer would be before I asked the question (30+ years into this, I don't think she second guesses herself too often). It might not work the same way with your banker, but it does make sense to stack the deck in your favor. Part of that involves asking at the right time.

Getting a Business Loan

What Are Interest Rates Doing?

Rates for small business loans vary widely. When rates are low over-all, application costs are usually lower too. Before you visit your banker, research the current interest rates for the type of loan you want. That way, when you visit your banker, you'll know whether her bank is charging higher or lower interest rates than the average. Sir Francis Bacon said, "Knowledge is power." Chatting with your banker about a loan is a perfect example of when this is true. Know the markets before you sit down with your banker and you'll have more power to negotiate.

Can You Repay the Loan?

This isn't as easy a question to answer as you might think. Do-or-die situations are not the best time to visit your banker. Timing is seldom right for a brand new business; banks view them as too risky. Market factors can impact a small business's ability to repay a loan. What's more, if competition has pushed prices for your goods or services down, the interest rate on your loan could exceed your margins—making repayment problematic.

Apply at the Beginning of the Month

Believe it or not, the best time to apply for a loan is influenced by the time of the month. Although they don't consider themselves to be salespeople, the first of the month is when your banker is working to obtain new loan accounts. Sometimes this could even mean a better deal for you and your small business. The end of the month is when they're trying to close out and push through as many loans as they can. New loans that cross their desk at the end of the month are likely to be ignored (or will get less attention) as bankers try to get their already-outstanding loans funded.

These aren't hard-and-fast rules by any stretch of the imagination, but if you can improve your odds when talking to the bank, you may be one of the 10% who leaves the bank with a loan.

▓ **Tip** Apply for your loan at the beginning of the month. Bankers will be hungrier for new business then. At the end of the month they will be busy digesting the business they've rustled up.

One More Thing

Ultimately, the best time to apply for a loan is when you're prepared. If "your ducks are in a row," as my grandmother used to say, other timing considerations become secondary. In my opinion, your ability to repay the loan is the single most important timing consideration. With that in mind, I wrap up this chapter by covering the factors your banker considers as you prepare your business case. In other words, the reasons why you need the loan, how you're going to repay the loan, and what you'll do should something unforeseen happen:

- *Projected revenue:* Your banker will likely want to see that $A + B = C$. If he extends a line of credit or a term loan to your business, how is that infusion of cash going to impact your bottom line? For example, if you are borrowing to facilitate expansion, where will you spend the loan amount and what is your expected return? A small business owner I know wanted to expand into a new and bigger space. He wasn't looking for buckets of cash; actually it was a rather small loan by most people's standards. But the $10,000 he was looking for would allow him to lease a new space, and it included some cash for additional marketing to ensure they were also finding new customers. He could demonstrate a reasonable return on the investment and his loan was funded. $A + B = C$ is what your banker wants to see.

- *Projected expenses:* You banker will also want to know the total cost of your plans. If you can't justify your expenditure of borrowed money with a positive ROI (return on investment) that demonstrates your ability to repay your loan, you'll likely leave the bank empty handed. The world of finance is a world of projections, assumptions, and best guesses as much as anything else. If you're not prepared to show the bank what you expect to happen, the timing isn't right.

- *Having skin in the game:* You read about this in an earlier chapter, but it bears repeating. You banker wants to know the total cost of what you want to do and whether you've invested your own assets—that you have skin in the game.

- *If the market will respond:* Your banker will want to know that this isn't a crap shoot. Even when you've made some personal investment in this endeavor, if you can't convince your banker that the market will respond and you have a reasonable chance of success, they'll likely pass. Nobody likes to throw good money after bad, particularly your banker.

- *Having a contingency plan:* If things in the market turn south, what then? Contingency plans and risk-mitigation strategies resonate with bankers. If you can demonstrate that you have a plan should things go south, you'll have a better chance of securing the financing you need. What's more, it's always good to imagine "what if?" scenarios when you're looking to the future. It forces you to take off the rose-colored glasses and *realistically* look into your crystal ball.

Although it probably feels like the time is right when you *don't* need the loan (and you could be right), don't despair. Benjamin Disraeli, a British politician, writer, and aristocrat of the nineteenth century, said, "The secret of success in life is for a man to be ready for his opportunity when it comes." In other words, be prepared for your visit with the banker.

Summary

What's the best type of loan for your small business? It's still too early to tell. You've read about only two of the most common bank loans—you're just getting started. The next chapter talks about the maze that is the SBA (the Small Business Administration).

Navigating the Maze of the SBA

Are We There Yet?

When the U.S. government talks about small business, what they're saying might not be what we're hearing. They tend to look at small businesses differently than most of us do. You might be surprised to learn that Uncle Sam considers a $30 million company with over 200 employees a small business, but I doubt most Americans would. Needless to say, the financing needs of the local bookstore or barbershop around the corner are very different from a tech firm with hundreds of employees.

Nevertheless, Karen Mills,[1] head of the Small Business Administration, announced that during her tenure at the SBA, she oversaw $106 billion in loans to more than 193,000 small businesses and entrepreneurs. That included $30.5 billion in loan guarantees in 2011 and $30.25 billion in 2012.

It might be a little easier to get an SBA loan today than it was in 2008, but it's not a simple process by any standard. Let's take a deeper look.

---

[1]Mills stepped down from her position at the end of August, 2013.

Guaranteed Loan Programs

According to the SBA, they don't actually make loans. That's the job of your local bank or other lending institution. The SBA:

> [S]ets the guidelines for loans, which are then made by its partners (lenders, community development organizations, and microlending institutions). The SBA guarantees that these loans will be repaid, thus eliminating some of the risk to the lending partners. So when a business applies for an SBA loan, it is actually applying for a commercial loan, structured according to SBA requirements with an SBA guarantee. SBA-guaranteed loans may not be made to a small business if the borrower has access to other financing on reasonable terms.[2]

In other words, even if you receive an SBA loan, you will still be working with a local banker. And you are not eligible for an SBA loan if there are other reasonable alternatives. The goal of the SBA is to assume some of the risk associated with small business lending by guaranteeing a percentage of any particular loan. This reduces the risk to your bank.

Other Programs Offered by the SBA

The SBA's financial assistance programs aren't limited to their guaranteed loan programs. There are other programs designed to meet key financial needs:

- *Bonding program (surety bonds):* A surety bond is a three-party financial instrument among contractors, project owners, and someone who agrees to be responsible for the debt or obligation (a *surety*, who in this case is partially guaranteed by the SBA's Surety Bond Guarantee program). It bonds the contractor to comply with the terms and conditions of the contract. Should the contractor fail to perform as agreed, the surety assumes the contractor's responsibilities and ensures that the project gets completed. When the SBA assumes a percentage of any potential loss, this guarantee gives the surety an incentive to provide bonding for eligible contractors, strengthening the contractor's ability to obtain bonding and opportunities. The SBA can guarantee bonds for contracts up to $5 million in most instances or even up to $10 million, depending on the contract.

---

[2]http://www.sba.gov/content/what-sba-offers-help-small-businesses-grow

- *Venture capital program:* The SBA's Small Business Investment Company (SBIC) program is a public-private partnership created to help small businesses find access to the capital they need to fund growth. The SBA doesn't invest directly in small businesses. Instead, it invests in private investment funds licensed as SBICs and supplements the capital they raise with access to low-cost, government-guaranteed debt. These SBICs operate much the same way as traditional venture capital firms, but they limit their investments to qualified small businesses as defined by the SBA.

To apply for an SBA loan, start at a bank in your area that participates in SBA programs. Don't assume they all do, because they don't. You still want to consider whether they specialize or have experience with your industry. Additionally, SBA guaranteed loans are structured to meet certain requirements to be eligible for the program. At the end of this chapter, there is a copy of the SBA loan application checklist. It lists the forms and documents you and your lender need in order to create a loan package you can submit to the SBA.[3]

Starting and Expanding Businesses

There are a number of SBA loan products available, depending upon the type of business you operate and your loan objectives. To make it simple, I use the categories outlined by the SBA.

Basic 7(a) Loan Program

A 7(a) loan[4] is intended to help specific businesses financially and is the most popular SBA loan. It can be used for a variety of business purposes, but there are some restrictions. Some of the basic uses include the following:

- Long-term working capital to pay operational expenses, accounts payable, or to purchase inventory

- Short-term working capital, including seasonal financing, contract performance, construction financing, and exporting

---

[3]The list is current as of this printing and is subject to change by the SBA at any time. You can find the most current list at www.SBA.gov.
[4]http://www.sba.gov/content/use-7a-loan-proceeds

- Revolving funds based on the value of existing inventory and receivables (under certain conditions)

- Equipment, machinery, furniture, fixtures, supplies, or materials

- Real estate, including land and buildings

- New building construction or renovation on an existing building

- Funds to establish a new business, contribute to the purchase of an existing business, or expand an existing business

- Funds to refinance existing business debt under certain conditions

Proceeds from an SBA loan cannot be used for any of the following purposes:

- To refinance existing debt when the lender would sustain a loss and the SBA would take over that loss through financing

- To enable a partial change of business ownership or a change that wouldn't positively benefit the business

- To reimburse funds owed to any owner, including any equity or capital invested to provide a bridge to an SBA loan

- To pay any delinquent state or federal withholding taxes or any other funds that should be held in escrow

- To fund anything that would not be generally considered a sound business purpose as determined by the SBA

7(a) Loan Amounts, Fees, and Interest Rates

The SBA doesn't set a minimum loan amount, but $5 million is the maximum amount it will guarantee. The SBA reports that the average 7(a) loan amount in 2012 was $337,730.

The SBA charges a loan guarantee fee to the lending institution based upon the loan's maturity and the dollar amount guaranteed, not the total loan amount. The lender you work with has the option to pass that fee along to you at closing if they choose.

On any loan with a term of one year or less, the fee is 0.25% of the guaranteed portion of the loan. On loans with longer terms, the normal fee is 2% of the SBA-guaranteed portion on loans up to $150,000, 3% on loans of $150,000 to $700,000, and 3.5% on loans of more than $700,000. There is an additional fee of 0.25% on any guaranteed portion over $1 million.

The interest rate you pay is negotiated between you and the lender—subject to SBA minimums. Both fixed and variable rates are available. The maximum rate is based upon a base rate and an allowable spread. The SBA recognizes the following as acceptable base rates:

- The prime rate published in a daily national newspaper

- The London InterBank one month prime, plus 3%

- The SBA peg rate

A few definitions are probably in order here. The *prime rate* is probably the most widely used benchmark for setting interest rates. It originally indicated the interest rates banks offered to their best customers—those with the best credit. The basis for the prime rate is the *federal funds rate*, which is set by the Federal Reserve Board and is the rate commercial banks use to lend to each other. The prime rate is typically slightly lower or higher than 3% above the rate set by the Federal Reserve.

The *London InterBank Offered Rate* (LIBOR) is established much the same way. The British Banker's Association sets the rate on a daily basis and it's derived from a filtered average of the world's most creditworthy bank's interbank deposit rates for larger loans with maturities between 24 hours and a full year.

The SBA *peg rate* is similar to the LIBOR rate in how it's calculated. It's the weighted average of rates the U.S. federal government pays for loans with maturities similar to the average SBA loan. The amount of the spread is negotiatied between the lender and the borrower, which is added to the base rate.

Even though lenders are allowed to add a spread to these base rates, the maximum spread can be no more than 2.5% on loans with maturities shorter than seven years and no more than 2.75% with maturities seven years or longer. However, the spread on loans of less than $50,000, and loans that are processed through express procedures, have higher maximums.

The SBA Express program allows approved lenders to use their own documentation and procedures for an SBA guaranteed loan—making it possible for the borrower to get approved without waiting for SBA approval. As you might guess, the express procedures have the potential of shortening the process for small business borrowers.

CDC 504 Loan Program

A CDC (Certified Development Company) 504 loan is designed to provide growing businesses with long-term, fixed-rate financing for major assets like property and buildings.

A CDC is a nonprofit corporation set up to contribute to the economic development of a community. CDCs across the country work with the SBA and private-sector lenders to provide loans to small businesses in a position to help develop local economies by creating local jobs, for example. CDC loans are 100% guaranteed by the SBA, as opposed to the 7(a) loan program described previously (the SBA guarantees up to 85% on loan amounts of $150,000 or less and 75% on loan amounts over $150,000 on a 7(a) loan).

Some of the things a 504 loan can be used for include:

- The purchase of property, including existing buildings
- Physical improvements, including grading, street improvements, utilities, parking lots, and landscaping
- The construction of new facilities or modernizing, renovating, or converting existing facilities
- The purchase of long-term machinery and equipment

Proceeds from a 504 loan cannot be used for any of the following:

- Working capital or inventory
- Consolidating, repaying, or refinancing debt
- Speculating or investing in rental real estate

CDC 504 Loan Amounts, Fees, and Interest Rates

How the funds will be used and which of the following three categories the funds are intended to support determine maximum loan amounts:

- *Job creation:* The maximum loan amount for meeting a job creation criteria or community development goal is $1.5 million. Your business must create one job for every $65,000 provided by the SBA. Small manufacturers must have a $100,000 job-creation or job-retention goal.

- *Public policy:* The maximum loan amount for meeting a public policy goal is $2 million. According to the SBA, the following are examples of acceptable public policy goals:

    - Revitalizing a business district

    - Expanding exports

    - Expanding minority business development

    - Developing rural areas

    - Increasing productivity and competitiveness

    - Restructuring because of federally mandated standards or policies

    - Addressing changes necessitated by federal budget cutbacks

    - Expanding small business concerns owned and controlled by veterans

    - Expanding small businesses owned and controlled by women

- *Small manufacturing:* The maximum loan amount for small manufacturers is $4 million. To qualify for a $4-million 504 loan, your business must meet the definition of a small manufacturer[5] and accomplish one of the following:

    - Create or retain one job for every $100,000 guaranteed by the SBA[6]

    - Improve the economy of the locality or achieve one or more public policy objectives[7]

The assets being financed are typically used for collateral along with a personal guarantee of the principal owner(s). Loan terms of 10 and 20 years are available, with interest rates pegged to an increment above the current market rate for 5-year and 10-year U.S. Treasury issues. Fees are approximately 3% of the loan and may be financed with the loan.

---

[5]http://www.sba.gov/content/identifying-industry-codes
[6]Section 501(d)(1) of the Small Business Investment Act (SBI Act): http://thomas.loc.gov/cgi-bin/query/z?c111:S.3839:
[7]Sections 501(d)(2) or (3) of the SBI Act.

Microloan Program

Very small loans are available for newly established or growing small businesses. The SBA makes these funds available to nonprofit community-based lenders. A maximum of $50,000 is available to eligible borrowers. Applications and credit decisions are all made on the local bank level.

Microloans can be used for:

- Working capital
- Inventory or supplies
- Furniture or fixtures
- Machinery or equipment

Loan proceeds cannot be used to pay existing debts or to purchase real estate.

Loan-repayment terms vary according to several factors, including the amount of the loan, what the loan proceeds will be used for, requirements determined by the intermediary lender, and the needs of the borrower. The maximum allowed repayment term is six years.

Interest rates vary, depending upon the lender and the costs to the lender from the U.S. Treasury. These rates are normally between 8 and 13%.

■ **Tip**   At rates of between 8 and 13%, an SBA microloan shouldn't be at the top of your list. Exhaust other sources of money first.

Disaster Loans

Disaster loans come in a few different varieties.

Disaster Assistance Loans

These loans provide financial assistance to victims of disasters in a declared disaster area. Disaster loans can be used to repair or replace the following items damaged or destroyed in a natural disaster:

- Real estate
- Personal property
- Machinery and equipment
- Inventory
- Business assets

Economic Injury Loans

If your small business has experienced substantial economic injury in a declared disaster area, you could be eligible for an SBA Economic Injury Disaster Loan (EIDL). The SBA defines "substantial economic injury" as your business's inability to meet its obligations and to pay ordinary and necessary operating expenses. EIDLs are designed to provide working capital to help small businesses survive a national disaster until normal operations can be resumed.

The interest rates on EIDLs will not exceed 4% per year, with terms no longer than 30 years. The repayment term is determined by your ability to repay the loan. This type of financing is available only when the SBA determines there are no other options to obtain credit elsewhere.

Export Assistance Loans

The SBA offers a few loan products specifically to assist small businesses in the export business. These loans are targeted at businesses that need additional capital to support export opportunities. An export business enages in trading goods produced in the United States, and shipped to another country, for future sale or trade.

Export Express: To support export activities, the Export Express loan is designed to streamline the process for obtaining financing and lines of credit up to $500,000. Borrowers are bound by the lender's current loan-approval process, but exporters get access to the funds faster. The SBA provides an expedited eligibility review with a response in less than 24 hours.

Export Working Capital: This loan type is designed to provide working capital to exporters who are able to generate export business, but don't have the working capital to support the transactions.

International Trade: These are term loans designed for businesses that plan to start or continue exporting—and can also be used by exporters that have been negatively affected by competition from importers. The proceeds of the loan must enable the borrower to be in a better competitive position.

Veteran and Military Community Loans

Are you a veteran of the armed forces? If so, you have some additional options with the Patriot Express loan. There's also help for businesses that employ reservists who are called up for active duty, when that results in economic hardship.

Patriot Express

To be eligible for a Patriot Express loan, the business must be owned and controlled by eligible veterans and members of the military community who want to establish or expand their business. To the SBA, "owned" and "controlled by" means at least a 51% ownership in the small business.

Eligible military community members include:

- Veterans

- Service-disabled veterans

- Active-duty service members eligible for the military's Transition Assistance Program

- Reservists and National Guard members

- Current spouses of any of these, including any service member

- Widowed spouses of service members or veterans who died during service or of a service-connected disability

The maximum loan amount on any Patriot Express loan is $500,000 and can be used for the same purposes as a 7(a) loan, including start-up and expansion costs, equipment purchases, permanent working capital, and inventory or business-occupied real estate purchases. The option to access loan proceeds as a line of credit is also available, subject to the lender's terms.

There is no collateral requirement for loans under $25,000, but the same collateral requirements for other SBA loans apply up to $350,000. For loans over $350,000, lenders are required to obtain either all collateral or enough collateral so the value is equal to the loan amount.

The local SBA district office has a current list of Patriot Express lenders in your area.

Military Reservist Economic Injury Disaster Loan

The purpose of this loan is to assist small businesses to meet obligations they are now unable to meet because a key employee was called-up to active duty in their role as a military reservist.

The maximum loan amount available is $2 million and is limited to the actual injury as calculated by the SBA. The amount is also limited by business interruption insurance and whether the business owner has sufficient funds to operate. If the business is a major source of employment in the community, the SBA has the authority to waive the $2 million statutory limit.

The purpose of the loan is to recover lost income or profits and may not be used for regular commercial debt, to refinance long-term debt, or to expand business operations.

Businesses that have the ability to fund their own recovery are not eligible for this assistance. Federal law requires the SBA to perform an evaluation to ensure that no other source of funds is available to the business without creating undue hardship.

Collateral is required for any loan over $50,000. The SBA will not deny a loan if the borrower doesn't have sufficient collateral to ensure the entire loan amount, but it does require the borrower to pledge whatever collateral is available.

The interest rate is 4% with up to a 30-year term, based on the SBA's determination of the borrower's ability to repay the loan.

Improving the Odds of SBA Loan Success

As described earlier in this chapter, the SBA doesn't make loans; your local bank or other lender does. The SBA simply eliminates some of the risk so that the lender can approve your application with more confidence.

Although the SBA's mission is to eliminate some of the risk their lender partners take on, they don't treat the process like a trip to Vegas. Like any other banker, they are anxious to avoid any risk they can—which makes acquiring an SBA loan challenging for many small business owners. With that in mind, here are five ways to improve your chances:

- *Understand the jargon:* Make sure you know what you're talking about when you visit your banker to discuss a potential loan. The most popular and flexible SBA loan is the 7(a) loan described earlier in the chapter. Make sure you're familiar with and understand the definitions and descriptions of each of the loans described in this chapter.

- *Cross your T's and dot your I's:* Make sure you bring your business and personal financial statements, including tax returns, accounts receivable and accounts payable aging, a short business plan, and reference letters. Basically, bring anything that a banker might be interested in to ensure that you are a good loan prospect. You want to show the bank that you're a smart investment rather than a risky one. The background information allows bankers in the decision-making process who'll never meet you to get a complete picture of your business and your professionalism. Don't assume that your most recent tax return or P&L is sufficient—you will be making a sales presentation to the banker in an effort to convince him that you are a great candidate for an SBA loan.

- *Show that you have skin in the game:* Prior to 2008, it might have been a little easier to get an SBA loan, but it's still possible. Although the SBA might not require the entire loan to be collateralized, they do expect the borrower to put up all the collateral they have, including equity in your home. As you might expect, this scares off some prospective borrowers. If your business has enough assets to put forward as collateral, you're in good shape. If not, you'll likely be required to use your home or other personal assets.

- *Be prepared to answer the tough questions:* Although industry success averages might not apply to you, your banker will want to know what *your* odds of success are. Most industry groups supply that kind of information to their members. If you feel like your business idea is doing (or will do) better than the industry average, your banker will want to know why you think that way. Remember, when all is said and done, bankers want to avoid risk. The more information you provide that helps them do that, the better your chances of success.

- *Avoid the very appearance of risk:* If you have a good business plan and can make a good case for an SBA loan, the last thing you want to do is give your banker the idea that you are willing to make risky decisions (even if they are calculated risks). Traditional lenders hate risk—and the SBA works with traditional lenders.

▓ **Tip** You don't want your banker to perceive you, or the reason you want funds, as risky in any way, shape, or form. Show your banker that you are trustworthy, and that your plan for the money makes good financial sense.

SBA Loan Application Checklist

Use this checklist to compile all the documents and other information you'll need in order to submit a compelling application. Nevertheless, if there is additional information that will help the bank and the SBA better understand your business and your ability to turn an SBA loan into business profit, by all means add those documents to this list.

- *SBA loan application:* Use the application for a business loan—SBA Form 4.[8]

- *Personal background and financial statement:* The SBA requires you to complete a statement of personal history—SBA Form 912[9]—and personal financial statement—SBA Form 413.[10]

- *Business financial statement:* Your business financial statement should demonstrate your ability to repay the loan. Prepare and include the following:

  - *Profit and loss (P&L) statement:* This must be current within 90 days of your application. You will also need to include any supplementary schedules from the last three fiscal years.

  - *Projected financial statements:* Include a one-year detailed projection of income and expenses, along with a written explanation of how you plan to achieve these objectives.

- *Ownership and affiliations:* Disclose any other businesses you have a financial interest in, including subsidiaries and affiliates, as well as any business you have a controlling interest in, in addition to any stock ownership, franchises, proposed mergers, and so on.

- *Business certificate/business license:* You need to provide your original business license or certificate of doing business. If you run a corporation, stamp your corporate seal on the SBA loan application form.

- *Loan application history:* Include records of any loans you have applied for in the past.

---

[8]http://www.sba.gov/content/application-business-loan
[9]http://www.sba.gov/content/statement-personal-history
[10]http://www.sba.gov/content/personal-financial-statement

- *Income tax returns:* Include signed personal and business federal tax returns from the previous three years (for all principals in the business).

- *Resumes:* Include a personal resume for each principal in the business.

- *Business overview and history:* Provide a brief written history of the business. Include successes as well as challenges, along with an explanation of why you are applying for an SBA loan.

- *Business lease:* Include a copy of your business lease, if you are renting property, that explains the terms of the lease (a note from your landlord will also work).

- *If you are purchasing an existing business:* If you're purchasing an existing business, you also need to include the following:

  - Current balance sheet and P&L of the business to be purchased

  - The previous two years federal income tax returns of the business

  - Proposed bill of sale, including terms of sale

  - Asking price with schedule of inventory, including machinery, equipment, furniture, and fixtures

Summary

Although the SBA is not the only source of financing for Main Street business owners, the interest rates and terms are some of the most attractive for traditional financing. Larger banks and community banks are part of the network of SBA lenders, and you should investigate more than one lender before jumping into what is typically a months-long process.

Last year the SBA made approximately $30 billion in loan guarantees to small business owners. One of the success stories highlighted by the SBA is PeakEnergy LLC.[11]

---

[11]http://www.sba.gov/content/small-business-owner-receives-sba-loan-working-capital

Steve Elsea, the business owner, helps utility companies and other energy providers access existing generators at private businesses during peak periods of demand. He used an SBA loan to develop proprietary software and purchase the hardware to interface with the generators. The hardware/software combination allows the energy providers to control the multiple standby generators from their respective dispatch centers.

Thousands of other borrowers from all across the country in many different industries take advantage of the SBA loan guarantee programs to start new businesses, expand existing businesses, and assist businesses that suffer the consequences of natural disasters every year.

Angels and Venture Capital

The Myth of the Shark Tank

There's a lot of talk in the media about venture capital (VC), usually associated with startups. Television makes it look like VC firms and angel investors are lining up to take your great idea and give you the money you need to get it going. Although there might be investors looking for something like your business, the truth is, an angel or VC firm is typically looking for a sexy tech startup that could turn into the next Facebook—not your Main Street business.

Although only about two percent of small businesses actually have what the VCs are looking for, no discussion of capitalizing Main Street business owners would be complete without addressing the topic. Hopefully by the end of this chapter, you'll have a good idea of whether VC funding is right for you.

What Is a Venture Capital Firm?

Venture capital is usually an investment of funds into early-stage, high-potential startups that offer some kind of unique technology. Unlike a loan, the venture capital fund makes money by owning equity in the companies in which they invest. Most of the time, the VC isn't involved in the early stages of a company's lifecycle,[1] but participates in what is usually called a *growth round* of funding.

---

[1]That's more the role of the angel, to be discussed later in the chapter.

Because their investment buys equity in the business, the payoff takes place when the business is either sold or goes public in an IPO (Initial Public Offering). Unlike a loan, VC funding doesn't require a monthly payment, but it usually does require the business owner to relinquish some ownership (sometimes even a controlling interest) in their business. I often chuckle at the small business owners on ABC's *Shark Tank*, who want the financial backing of Barbara Corcoran, Kevin O'Leary, or Mark Cuban, but don't want to give up any ownership.

Years ago I had a close friend who was able to attract some interest in his business by some potential equity investors who were convinced they could turn his small business into a multimillion-dollar company. At the time he had other partners, but he maintained the controlling interest in his company. When they finally came to terms, his ownership went from around 70% to 10%. He remained the president of the company, but he now had a major shareholder with an incredible amount of clout when it came time to make decisions.

When I asked him why he was willing to give up so much to an equity investor, he showed great savvy for such a young guy. "Right now I have a big huge piece of a really small pie," he said. "Although I might have a much smaller piece of the pie, it's going to be a very big pie."

Not too many years later, he proved me right when his business sold. He was living the dream and walked away with somewhere between $10 and $20 million. He knew his new equity partners had the industry knowledge to take his business to the next level and make some serious money. For him, it was worth giving up all that equity.

Even if your business is something a VC is interested in, you might not want to give up ownership, but there are a lot of entrepreneurs who do.

This is something you need to determine for yourself, but it's been reported that venture capital accounts for about 2% of U.S. Gross Domestic Product[2] (U.S. GDP) and creates a lot of jobs for high-tech businesses in the growth phase of their businesses. According to the National Venture Capital Association, 11% of private sector jobs come from venture-backed companies.[3]

---

[2] "Venture Impact: The Economic Importance of Venture-Backed Companies to the U.S. Economy." Nvca.org. Retrieved 2012-05-18.
[3] *Venture Impact* (5th ed.). IHS Global Insight, 2009, p. 2. ISBN: 0-9785015-7-8.

The Pitfalls of VC Funding

I don't think giving up equity is necessarily a pitfall if the investors have the savvy and wherewithal to help you build a thriving and growing business. My concerns are at more of a basic philosophical level.

Knowing ahead of time that VC companies don't reap the rewards of their investment until a businesses is sold or goes public, you should realize that the focus of your new business partner is to flip your company for as big a return as they can as quickly as they can. That's the way they and *their* investors make profits. Very few—and I'm not aware of any—are willing to invest in companies for the long term. If you want to build a company that will last 100 years or more, you likely won't be very appealing to an equity investor (even though that will make you a very appealing business generally).

Other than my personal distaste for what is sometimes called "taco chip" companies—companies with a long-term value of a taco chip—there are a few challenges associated with venture funding. Most of time, they aren't content with earning interest rates on par with bank rates. They want a little more. Here are a few examples:

- *Management position:* Most of the time, VCs want to be added as a member of your company's executive team. You might not look at it this way, but they want to ensure that your company is headed down a path that will reap their anticipated financial reward.

- *Funds might not immediately be available:* Unlike a traditional term loan, the promised funds might not immediately be available. Many VCs set goals and milestones for the release of funds. Most of the time, funding is released in stages and is usually allocated for growth and expansion. I'm editorializing here, but expansion with an eye toward sale or public offering might not always be the best kind of growth.

- *The term "equity" funding implies that you will be giving up equity for funding:* Most VC firms require you to give up an equity position. It won't be small potatoes either. It's not uncommon to see a VC firm looking for 60% or greater, depending on the investment.

- *Your business plan could become public:* When you approach a bank or other small business finance company, it's customary to expect that they will sign a non-disclosure agreement regarding your business plan and what you want to do. This is seldom the case with venture funding. VCs almost always refuse to sign such agreements.

- *Decisions might not be yours to make any longer:* At least you won't have carte blanche to make decisions. One of the biggest challenges faced when accepting venture funds is giving up many of the key decisions you would otherwise make. VCs usually want a lot of influence over key decisions—and they don't always agree with the founder. Their equity position gives them a seat at the table when it's time to make important decisions.

That being said, there are benefits to working with VC firms. Many of which have the potential to turn a young, struggling startup into an incredibly profitable business.

 Tip Make sure the goals you have for your company and the goals your potential investor have for your company are compatible.

Benefits of VC Funding

If you have a business that might be interesting to a venture firm, you could have access to an incredible amount of business savvy to help you succeed:

- *Management consulting could be part of the package:* I don't think it's any secret that not all entrepreneurs are good business managers. Great ideas, a strong business plan, and a killer product don't always come from the same entrepreneur with the skills to successfully run a business. If you don't have those skills or you don't have a partner who does, a VC interested in your company could fill the gap. Because most VC firms will have equity in your firm, their desire to help manage your company could be a boon to entrepreneurs who don't have those skills.

- *Specific business discipline expertise can help you ramp things up:* Many VC firms have expert business consultants on their payroll who can help with things like marketing, distribution, research, and more. Having an open channel to an organization filled with the expertise your organization might lack can improve your ability to compete in your space. I once worked with a number of highly qualified people from Harvard and MIT who were at our disposal as part of our company's VC firm. We often turned to them for research into our market and advice on special projects. They were a great resource. Looking back, I don't think we took advantage of that expertise as much as we could have.

- *Human resource expertise and recruiting capability:* Recruiting key talent is a challenge for startups and young firms looking to grow. Many VC firms can help you find people with the specialized skills needed to help your business grow. Some firms even have HR people to help the companies they've invested in staff key rolls. This can be of huge benefit to business owners who want to mitigate the risks associated with hiring the wrong people for key rolls.

- *But wait, there's more:* Starting a business, or taking a young company to the next level, is not for the faint hearted. Legal concerns, payroll matters, and tax issues are just a few of the concerns faced as a company grows. It's not uncommon for a venture firm to take an interest in providing resources to help deal with these issues, because they have a vested interest in your success.

Although your banker or other financing source has an interest in your success—they certainly don't want you to default on your loan—because a VC firm has invested in your future, they're likely going to do everything they can to ensure that you succeed in a timely matter.

Equity funding is basically exchanging capital for ownership in your business. It isn't right for everyone.

Before You Pitch Your Business to a VC

Even if you find yourself within the two percent of small businesses a venture fund might be interested in, don't expect them to come knocking on your door. More than likely you'll need to sell them on the idea. Before you start looking through the phone book for your local VC firm, there are a few concepts you need to have nailed down. As obvious as these questions sound, you might be surprised at how many small business owners don't have their ducks in a row.

What's Your Elevator Pitch?

I once attended a local Q&A with some pretty experienced entrepreneurs who, when asked, couldn't explain what their company did. I'm not suggesting they didn't know, they just couldn't articulate it very well. Before you pitch a venture capitalist, you better have your elevator pitch down.

I like the idea of starting with a piece of paper or a Word document. This gives you a chance to live with it, change it, and clearly identify what you do. Start with a page. Take the full page or two—somewhere around 600 or 700 words—to describe what you do. Work with the page for a few days; make sure you've accurately described what you do and why.

Once you're done with the page, move on to the next step—the paragraph. The challenge here is to distill the essence of everything you've written into 100 words or less. Live with it for a while; make sure you've written a good description and then move to the next step—the sentence. By this time you've likely noticed that writing the paragraph was decidedly more difficult that writing the page. Expect the sentence to be even more difficult. This is what many people call your *elevator pitch*.

If you can't articulate what you do in a single sentence that puts a spotlight on your unique idea, you're not ready to pitch your idea to a VC firm. What's more, if you haven't written the page and distilled it down to a paragraph, you probably won't be able to accurately describe what you do in a sentence. Working through the exercise is valuable, even if you never refer to the page or paragraph again. However, I'm pretty sure you will.

Do You Know Your Market?

Most products or services are designed to address a need in the market. Can you clearly articulate that need? What is the problem you're trying to solve? Do your potential customers recognize the problem? What are they willing to pay to solve the problem? Will *your* product actually solve the problem?

Years ago, as a much younger version of myself, I was job hunting and was ultimately recruited by a major insurance company. Although I knew life insurance was a tough way to make a living, I also knew that people who were good at it made a lot of money. I was interested enough that I was giving it some serious consideration. My brother-in-law had successfully sold insurance for a while, so I gave him a call to see what he thought of the company. I was surprised by his response.

"Ty, if you want to be a salesperson, why not sell something people either know they need or something that most people want. Life insurance isn't either one."

He then explained that most of the people I would talk to wouldn't give the purchase of life insurance the importance it deserved and I would likely spend most of my time trying to explain why it was important. "When was the last time you called up a life insurance salesperson and asked her to come tell you about her product?" he asked.

Bottom line—if you have a product or service that doesn't resonate with your market (even if it's a fantastic product), a VC firm isn't going to be interested in what you have to offer.

Who Are You Talking To?

In marketing terms, this is the first and most important question you need to ask yourself. Many companies spend countless hours defining the who. I'm a big fan of articulating who my buyer (in this case, the VC) is, who influences the buying decision, and who the user of my product will likely be. Odds are they are not the same person. If you can accurately and persuasively articulate "who," you greatly increase the odds of a successful pitch—especially when you have a product that resonates with the market and solves a real market need, and have potential customers who will pay for your solution.

Having spent a good portion of my career in marketing, I'm always surprised to see how many companies can't identify "who" they're talking to. They have a good idea, but they don't spend the time to make sure they know. Remember, if you're courting venture funding, you're looking for a partner. They want to know that your company knows who they're products are designed for.

Is this VC Firm Right for You?

Once you know your market, you know how to articulate what your product does, and you know who your customers or potential customers are, you're still not quite done. You need to prepare your pitch and make sure you're ready to do the "song and dance." However, the pitch process is also a great time to make sure *you* want to work with *them*.

Lendio founder and CEO Brock Blake talks about the process he went through with Lendio. Blake is a pretty dedicated family man and makes sure he sets aside time to spend with his wife and children. I wish I had been as dedicated to this idea when I was his age. He often talks about how we dedicate time to those things we think are most important—and for him, it's his family.

During a meeting with a potential VC investor, the investor said something like, "I don't know how you can have a family and still be an entrepreneur. To be successful, you just have to dedicate way too much time focused on work. A family just isn't compatible with that."

Because Blake's primary focus is his family, this was a huge red flag—this particular investor just wasn't right for him and his business.

Sometimes small business owners are so focused on raising a successful round of venture funds, they don't ask themselves the critical question, "Do I really want to work with these guys?" Remember, taking money from a VC is different than taking out a loan at the bank. You're taking on a new partner—a partner with a lot of say regarding how you run your business.

■ **Tip**　Don't ignore the importance of your pitch to any potential VC. You may need to customize every presentation for each specific VC. Taking shortcuts with your pitch will handicap your ability to find the funding you need.

Pitching Your Business to a Venture Firm

Although every venture firm is a little different, there are some common things they all seem to look for. In addition to your understanding of the market, your customers, and the problem you solve, they'll also want to know or hear about:

- *The team:* Who is your leadership team and why are they qualified to execute your idea? Is the organization you've built more capable than your top four or five competitors? They'll want visibility into work history, networks, skills, and any previous successes.

- *Demo:* Most VCs insist on a demonstration, or "demo," that shows how your product works. Investors want to make sure they understand how your product works compared to similar products they may already be familiar with before they invest. At the very least they'll want to see a mockup.

- *Business model:* How does your business make money? Who pays? How much do they pay? And, when do they pay?

- *Your competition:* Do you know everyone who could be considered a competitor? Do you know what they're offering to address your market? Are they successful? A VC will want a list of competitors with some analysis of what you believe they are doing right and where you think they are weak. What are your competitive advantages?

- *Financial overview:* What are your expected revenues and expenses? How long do you anticipate this round of funding to last?

- *Funding:* How much capital are you trying to raise, and what are you going to do with it? Are you looking for money to develop your team, for overhead, or to expand?

- *The future:* What is your vision for the future? Have you established milestones for the next two or three years? Most VC firms will keep track of those milestones and hold you accountable for meeting them.

Although there is nothing more exciting than the phone call or e-mail that lets you know you have a new VC partner, having a good idea isn't enough to make it happen. Many entrepreneurs aren't prepared to answer some of these hard questions and wind up stumbling right out of the gate. If venture funding makes sense for you and your business, with a little bit of preparation, you'll improve your odds of success.

Many VCs are located near major universities or in the high-tech centers of the country like Silicon Valley, New York, and Boston. You can search online, where there are a number of directories. Before you reach out to a venture firm, do enough research to know whether the VC you're interested in working with will be interested in you and your type of business.

Don't be afraid to talk to others in your industry where they obtained their financing, if they are venture-backed. Referrals can make it much easier to get a meeting with a VC.

The Angel Down the Street: When Local Investors Come to the Rescue

Angel investors are typically affluent individuals who provide capital for small business ideas they personally believe in. Like a VC, they are typically looking for an equity position, but they will sometimes provide capital in the form of a private business loan.

Although the term originates from Broadway, where wealthy individuals provided money needed to fund theatrical productions, it's used in a broader context now. Many "angels," as they are sometimes called, tend to devote their wealth to fund businesses and initiatives that are of personal interest or represent an industry familiar to the investor.

Unlike VCs, angel investors use their own funds to invest—which can make them expensive. Depending upon the investor, funds can range from a few thousand to millions of dollars.

Where to Look for Angel Investors

Angels are usually in larger metropolitan areas and can be hard to find, but looking in the right *types* of places is a good start:

- *Colleges and universities:* Many angels like to watch the technological developments that come out of major universities. A good place to look for angel investors is an entrepreneurship program supported by a local university.

- *Business incubators:* There are hundreds of business incubators all across the country that offer entrepreneurs inexpensive rent, access to shared services, and the opportunity to work with successful business professionals in an atmosphere of entrepreneurship. Some of these incubators also offer formal access to angel investors.

- *VC clubs:* Because of the success of many high-tech firms, large numbers of angel investors have started to formalize their efforts by creating investment groups or clubs. These people are actively looking for ventures to invest in and want to hear from entrepreneurs with the next great idea.

- *Angel confederacies:* Some angels don't like the idea of formalized investments within the confines of a VC club, but nevertheless band together within informal groups to discuss potential deals and share information. Although many of them prefer to invest individually, they sometimes will join together for specific opportunities. These groups aren't easy to find, but once you meet one of them, you'll likely have access to them all.

A great place to start looking for these groups might be with a call to your local chamber of commerce, because these investors often have a connection to the chamber. You can also reach out to your accountant, your attorney, or even a VC firm. You might also be able to find the information you need by talking to your banker.

I was speaking with a couple of bankers recently. They both mentioned how angels and VC firms were taking some of the small business loan business away from their bank. Although they didn't seem too happy about it, they acknowledged that many of the people who couldn't get funding through a traditional bank loan because they were either very young companies or startups were finding success with equity financing.

I have to admit, I wouldn't have thought equity funding would be much of a competitor for the bank, but they even suggested that some large banks were offering VC services. I have heard of a fairly large bank in Oklahoma that recently purchased a very large alternative funding company a couple of months ago. They felt like it enhanced the small business lending services they could offer to business owners who might otherwise leave their bank looking for options someplace else.

Summary

In most cases, funding from angels or venture capitalists isn't in the cards for Main Street business owners. The following chapters discuss some unique and very specialized financing options that level the playing field for many small business owners.

The Sun Will Come Out Tomorrow

You Have Options

The last few chapters discussed the challenges associated with financing your small business at the bank and how only 10% of Main Street business owners actually leave the bank with the financing they're looking for. You read about what I call the "myth of the shark tank" and learned why so few businesses attract a venture capitalist or angel investor.

If you've been turned down by a bank (which might be why you're reading this book), you're certainly not alone. What's more, you still have options. I think the hardest part for most Main Street business owners is facing the reality that the bank isn't interested in them and that they need to find alternative sources of financing. If you find yourself walking back to the car rejected by your banker, take an honest look at where you are and consider your options.

Remember, you *do* have options.

Over the last several years, many small business lenders have entered the market, which is good news for small business borrowers. These are smaller community bankers who understand the importance of a healthy small business community or single-branch banks that serve a limited geographic area. In addition, many non-bank lenders have entered the market in recent days.

These lenders typically specialize in different types of loans. They include commercial real estate lenders, factoring companies, credit card issuers, merchant cash advance lenders, and even lenders who specialize in franchise loans, or loans for women in buisness. You'll read about these in greater detail throughout the rest of this book.

Regardless of whether you go back to the bank that turned you down or decide to try one of the alternative lenders discussed throughout the book, you should start with what you're presenting to the lender. Although alternative lenders are unlikely to hold you to the same standards as your local bank, they do expect you to be prepared to talk about your business, including what you intend to do with the proceeds of your loan and how you plan to repay it.

With that in mind, let's revisit some of the information you need to prepare your loan "package."

■ **Tip** Alternatives to a loan from the local bank might be in places that small business owners wouldn't normally investigate. Keep your mind open; the chapters to come discuss many alternatives.

Preparing Your Loan Package

Since the following information applies to any type of loan you might need—traditional bank loan or alternative financing—I describe a typical loan package. Your lender might not need all of this information, but it certainly doesn't hurt to be prepared.

Because there is a substantial amount of paperwork associated with this process, you need to give some thought as to how you'll organize your paperwork. I suggest a professional-looking notebook with sections divided by tabs, including a table of contents. The goal is to make it as easy as possible for the loan officer to find all the information she needs to process your application. The easier you make it for her, the more likely your application will get the attention it deserves.

■ **Tip** Come to the loan meeting with a professional-looking binder. It should contain all the information required for the lender to answer any/all questions about your application. It will also reflect well on you.

You might be interested to know that most loan officers don't have the luxury of technology to help them through the loan process. Much of the paperwork is created and managed manually, which can make smaller loan amounts expensive to process. One lender confided to me that loan amounts under $250,000 were difficult for his bank because the paperwork was so expensive it wasn't worth the effort. It's true that alternative lenders often do larger (and smaller) loans, but their bread and butter is often in the $40,000 to $50,000 range.

In addition to a tabbed binder of some kind, you might also want to think about scanning or otherwise including these same documents digitally. The digital soft copy will allow your loan officer to easily print any extra copies he might need for others involved in the decision-making process.

Here's a rundown of what you need in your loan package.

The Loan Summary

The loan summary should be the first section of your loan package. This document should stand alone and act as an executive summary of your loan proposal. It should be designed to create interest in your loan request. Think of the loan summary the same way you think of an executive summary of a business plan. It should include all the facts of the overall loan package. It's best to create the loan summary after you've compiled the completed package. That way you don't forget anything.

Typical loan summary contents:

- Company information
- Project description
- Company/project principal's experience summary
- Sources and uses of funds
- Requested loan terms
- Summary of assets and collateral
- Project financial summary
- Current company/project financial summary

Loan Package Format

Here's what you need in the rest of the package:

- *A description of your business:* Include background information regarding how long you've been in business, and be sure to list all the owners. (For example: "My parents are not only my parents, they are also my business partners." A lender wants to know all the players in the business who have *any* ownership.)

- *The amount you are seeking and the reason(s):* This may be obvious, but the lender wants to know the amount you're looking for, what you plan on doing with it, your plans for repayment, and any collateral that you can use to secure the loan (remember, lenders like to see skin in the game).

- *Profiles of the business owners:* Lenders, even alternative ones, like to mitigate risk as much as possible, so your lender will want to know the credentials of all the owners, their experience, and the roles they play within the organization. Your lender will likely also want to see their personal financial history— including income tax statements, credit references, and a list of debt they carry.

- *A detailed description of your product or service:* Along with the description of your product or service, include a list of materials required to produce your product and any information you have regarding consumer demand. Remember, the goal is to give lenders anything that will make it easier for them to approve your loan. The more information they have, the better they'll be able to understand and mitigate the risks associated with working with you.

- *Forms and other paperwork:* Before you submit your package, make sure you have all the applicable forms, including:

  - Any lease or mortgage agreements

  - Proof of insurance coverage

  - Profit-and-loss statements for the most recent three years

- Business federal income tax statements for the past five years

- Cash flow statements for a minimum of two years

- Copies of any licenses or permits

- Assessment of any inventory or equipment

- *Market research:* Because so many businesses fail, your lender will probably ask you to demonstrate that you have a complete understanding of your business and the market. He will want to see any demographic research you've done, including why you think your product or service resonates with the marketplace, whether it meets a market need, if it's something your customers are willing to pay for, and how you intend to market/sell to them.

- *Industry analysis:* Include what you know about your competition. List all of your competitors, including their addresses, how close they are to your business, their products or services, and how they compare to you (see the following sidebar, "Performing a SWOT Analysis").

- *Use of funds:* Provide an outline of what you intend to do with the funds and what you expect the impact to be. A loan that facilitates growth is usually treated more favorably than a loan intended to keep your business afloat.

- *Breakeven analysis:* If your business is profitable and the loan is intended to capture additional market share, increase capacity, or hire additional employees, make that clear. If your business is not currently profitable, you need to indicate when you expect profits to equal expenses.

PERFORMING A SWOT ANALYSIS

A *SWOT* (strengths, weaknesses, opportunities, and threats) analysis helps identify the strengths and weaknesses of your business and of your competition. It helps illuminate opportunities to capture additional market share. It also helps you identify where your competition might capture market share from you.

— Strengths: Ways in which your product or service is superior to the competition.

— Weaknesses: Ways in which your product or service needs improvements to compete better with its competitors.

— Opportunities: Advantages that you can exploit to capture additional market share.

— Threats: Situations, competitors, or products that could be a threat to your market position.

Why Alternative Lenders Might Be Better for You

Part of the reason that lending to very small businesses is so difficult for community bankers is because these businesses are competing for attention with firms doing up to $35 million in annual revenues and up to 1,500 employees. Because the SBA considers such companies small businesses, so does your local bank.

Although political candidates love to talk about how they're trying to help the local plumber, hair salon, mechanic, or other Main Street business (the kind of establishments most Americans identify as small businesses), they're actually doing the most good for the bigger firms described previously.

What's more, after the financial meltdown of 2008, many banks abandoned the Main Street business owners who had been their bread-and-butter customers and moved upstream to service more established businesses looking for larger loan amounts.

Part of that decision is due to regulatory restrictions regarding whom they can lend to, but another part of the decision is due to the cost of underwriting and processing the loans. Despite the technology that otherwise permeates the way we communicate with each other, interact with our favorite companies, and keep in touch with our customers and friends, bankers are still using manual processes when making decisions about your business and funding your small business loan. That means it's just as expensive to process the $45,000 loan amount commonly requested by business owners on Main Street as it is to process the $250,000 or more loans needed to finance the working capital and growth needs of bigger firms.

Despite the negative impact on their local communities, it's hard to blame the banker who chooses to lend to the $20 million dollar software company looking for $500,000 to increase their marketing efforts and hire another 200 or so employees instead of Jimmy's Barbershop because Jimmy needs $10,000 to remodel his barbershop and upgrade to a new barber chair.

That's not to say your local community bank (or even a community bank across the country) is never a good place to get a loan. Some savvy bankers have decided that doing business online is a good idea and they are working hard to make their small business loan products attractive to business owners who might never step into their bank. Some of them focus their online efforts within their current geographical footprint, but that's not true of all of them. In fact, over the last couple of years many bankers are jumping into online small business lending regardless of where the business is located.

Just What Is an Alternative Lender?

In fairness, *alternative lender* is a pretty broad term used to describe any non-bank lender. Although they have been considered financing resources of last resort by some business owners, as more and more alternative lenders enter the market to fill the vacuum left by the traditional banks, their terms and rates are getting more competitive.

I think this is a good thing for the roughly 90% of Main Street business owners who end up leaving the bank empty-handed.

Alternative lenders turn to often overlooked sources of collateral to secure a loan to a small business owner—real estate, accounts receivables, or even the monthly volume of credit card transactions. I don't want to imply that your credit rating isn't important to these lenders. It is, but it's not the go/no-go metric used at most banks. Alternative lenders are typically more flexible than banks regarding repayment terms and loan-approval requirements. What's more, they're often much faster at processing your paperwork and funding your loan—hours or days as opposed to weeks or months. I recently spoke to one lender that prides itself on the number of loans they're able to fund before the end of the day.

Some of these loan types have been around for hundreds of years. Much of the early exploration of the new world was funded by this type of investment financing, and although interest rates are typically higher than with traditional term loans, these lenders fill the gap for many Main Street business owners who don't qualify for traditional bank loans. What's more, although they do sometimes deal with much larger amounts, their bread and butter is the smaller loan amounts that Jimmy's Barbershop or Bert's Plumbing are looking for.

I recently spoke with a small book publisher who needed some cash to print a children's book for a seasonal promotion. With a $35,000 advance on his monthly credit card transactions, he was able to go to market, meet his customer demand, capture a substantial profit, and repay his loan over the space of about six weeks. Had he relied on his local bank instead of non-traditional financing, he probably would have still been waiting for approval over the same six weeks. The quicker access to funding makes it possible to ramp up quickly and capture revenue that might otherwise be lost.

Note   Alternative lenders can supply you with the money you need far faster than most local banks.

A reputable alternative lender is happy to sit down with you to discuss your particular financing needs and determine the best fit for your situation. A one-size-fits-all approach to this type of lending doesn't fit, so make sure you ask questions and understand what you're signing up for.

Regrouping and Rethinking Your Desire for a Loan

Although non-traditional or alternative funding is sometimes a nearly perfect solution for a specific situation, turning to a merchant cash advance or other type of alternative financing to satisfy a long-term capital need is usually too expensive in the long haul. Too often, "hope-ium" and optimism get confused and business owners think that an influx of cash will solve *all* of their problems. Perhaps instead, there are some fundamental issues within the business that you need to address before you try to get a loan. Sometimes just because you *can* get a loan with an alternative lender doesn't mean you *should*.

There are times when a loan is not a good idea. Sometimes the higher interest rates and terms of financing are simply too expensive. What's more, there are situations when financing of any kind just isn't a good idea.

If you're in any of the following situations, you might want to regroup and ask yourself whether financing your venture now is a good idea. In these cases, your business might be better served by exercising patience and waiting before borrowing:

- *Your business is only an idea and not yet a business:* You may have a really great idea for a business, but if that's all you have, a loan probably isn't a good idea right now. As already discussed, the bank wants to see a few years of business records, and ideas don't create credit card receipts or accounts receivables, so a merchant cash advance or accounts receivable factoring isn't a realistic possibility. There are hard asset lenders, who are willing to take any hard assets you or your business own (jewelry, luxury cars, watches, equipment, and so on) and lend against a percentage of the value of those items, but you should consider them the same way you consider a pawn loan. They insist on holding your asset and the interest rate is untenable as a long-term solution.

  If this describes your situation, you may need to turn to family, friends, or some sort of crowd-funding to secure financing. You might also consider finding a partner with the ability to fund your venture. However, regrouping and waiting until you have business income that you can secure a loan with is likely the best answer.

- *You have no business income:* Even if you have assets to borrow against, unless your product or service is going to be the next Facebook or Instagram, it might not be a good idea to put your assets at risk. I know there are a lot of small business owners who have pulled rabbits out of their hats, but the odds are not in your favor. If you're getting your business started by taking on debt, remember you really are rolling the dice.

- *Your business is a startup and you have bad personal credit:* In this case, it's very unlikely you will ever get a loan. You need to spend the next 12 months rebuilding your credit and getting some legs under your business. Of course, there are payday loans and hard asset loans, but you need to accept that you won't get a loan from a bank. Unless you are doing enough business to have other assets that an alternative lender would consider as collateral, there is *no* loan in your immediate future. The good news is, once your credit improves and you have another year or two under you, your odds of getting a loan dramatically improve.

■ Tip Don't take out a business loan unless you have income and a plan for repayment.

Summary

The following chapters outline many of the most popular alternative options available to small business owners looking for capital. As more and more non-bank lenders enter the market, more Main Street business owners are finding the resources they need to grow and thrive. Even better, as the market has become more competitive in the last few years, interest rates are coming down and terms are improving for small business owners.

Although the idea of turning to alternative lending sources for capital might not be something you would have considered in the past, there are thousands of small business owners who have successfully leveraged unique and different options to build very successful businesses. The challenge is for borrowers to get used to this new paradigm.

Asset-Based Lending

Need a Piece of New Equipment?

When you're applying for a loan, it helps to be specific. If the reason for the loan is to purchase machinery or tools (work vehicles, manufacturing tools, computer hardware/software, and so on) needed to conduct business, there are lenders willing to use the purchased equipment as collateral. Many lenders like these asset-based loans and will finance 100% of them.

You can also acquire loans against equipment your business already owns.

What Qualifies for an Equipment Loan?

For the purpose of an equipment loan, any tangible asset that is essential to a company's operations, and even equipment that is not essential but nonetheless necessary, qualifies. Equipment is generally moveable and may be more or less expensive than other fixed assets such as a building or real estate, but it is costly enough that it usually requires financing to purchase.

Trucks for transporting materials as well as telephones and computers are all examples of equipment. The forementioned examples of equipment might be integral to doing business while other items—counting scales, work benches, or a pallet jack—might not be integral, but could be considered necessary. So they also also qualify.

Every major bank—and many alternative lenders—offer equipment loans. Some lenders specialize in different types of equipment loans. There are asset loans specific to construction equipment, farming and ranching, and computers and other high-tech equipment.

Tip Tech companies, farmers, contractors, and others can all find loans customized for their industry. These more specialized loans take into consideration industry conditions that might not apply elsewhere.

How the SBA Approaches Equipment Loans

This section describes the SBA's CDC/504 loan program and explains how it applies to financing equipment. I briefly described this program earlier, in Chapter 5, but let's dig in a little deeper here.

To qualify for a CDC/504 loan, the small business must meet certain eligibility requirements that include the following:

- Must be a for-profit company

- Must do business in the United States

- Must have a net worth of less than $15 million and an average net income of less than $5 million after taxes for the last two years

- Cannot use the loan for speculation or rental real estate

- Must meet the general SBA eligibility requirements discussed in Chapter 5

- Must use the proceeds for an approved purchase— fixed assets like real estate or equipment

- Must not have funds available from other sources

- Must have the ability to repay the loan on time from the business' projected operating cash flow

- Must be able to demonstrate a historic willingness and ability to pay their debts and that they have abided by the laws of their community

- Must demonstrate relevant management expertise and experience

- Must have a feasible business plan in place

You can use proceeds from a CDC/504 loan to purchase equipment, machinery, land, and existing buildings. You can even use them to make improvements to property, including such projects as grading, updating utilities, paving parking lots, and landscaping. Proceeds from the loan can also be used for the construction of new facilities, modernizing aging facilities, renovating, or converting existing facilities.

Like most SBA loans designed for a specific purpose, loan proceeds cannot be used for working capital or inventory, consolidating or refinancing another debt, or speculating or investing in rental property.

As with any SBA loan, if you want to apply for a CDC/504 loan, you need to find a local SBA lender and complete the appropriate paperwork outlined in Chapter 5.

Tip A CDC/504 loan from the SBA can be a good deal—rates are pegged at slightly above the current yield on 5- and 10-year Treasury securities. The fee is 3% of the total amount, but that can be financed as well.

Other Types of Asset-Based Lending

Another way to acquire the equipment you need to operate your business is to lease instead of buy. There are options for leasing just about anything you need to operate a business—computers, heavy equipment, even complete offices. Whether you purchase or lease your equipment largely depends on the type of business and the nature of the equipment.

The Equipment Leasing Association of America claims that about 80% of U.S. companies lease some or all of the equipment they use. Depending on your circumstances, leasing can be problematic or can offer some pretty attractive advantages:

- There is usually a lower monthly payment when compared to a loan.

- You can get a fixed versus floating interest rate in some cases.

- Lease payments can generally be expensed rather than amortized, potentially reducing your taxes in the short term (you should consult your tax advisor to determine if that's the case for you).

- You may be able to avoid tying up cash flow with a down payment.

- You can utilize the most up-to-date business equipment.

■ **Note** In many cases, you can expense your lease payments rather than amortize the asset purchase over many years. This will reduce your taxes in the short term. Check with your accountant to ensure you can take advantage of the opportunity.

Of course, you should also consider some of the disadvantages:

- You will probably pay a higher price for the equipment in the long term (depending on the terms of the lease).

- You are making a commitment to keeping the equipment for at least the term of the lease, which can be problematic if your need for the equipment fluctuates or diminishes.

- If you decide to keep any leased equipment, you may need to purchase it after the lease terms are met.

Every lease decision is unique. Make sure you compare the short-term and long-term costs when determining whether to lease or purchase. You want to ask questions like:

- What is the cost of the lease?

- What am I saving as a result of the lease?

- How do those numbers compare to the cost of purchasing the equipment?

- What costs are associated with getting out of the lease early?

Much like the financing options available when purchasing equipment, there are many ways to acquire a lease:

- *Banks:* Not all banks offer equipment leasing, but the ones that do typically offer lower interest rates. Be sure to verify whether they service the lease after you've signed on the dotted line.

- *Equipment dealers:* In much the same way your auto dealer can finance your new car, equipment dealers can help you secure a lease on a new piece of equipment. They can also help you with other financing options. These agreements are usually with an independent leasing company.

- *Independent leasing companies:* Much like banks, independent leasing companies come in all shapes and sizes and offer a number of leasing options.

- *Captive leasing companies:* These are subsidiaries of the equipment manufacturers.

- *Brokers:* Much like mortgage or real estate brokers, brokers charge a fee to act as an agent between the lessor and the lessee. They are a small percentage of the market.

"Personal Asset" Lenders: Keep Your Eyes Wide Open

As banks and other traditional lenders tightened credit requirements over the last couple of years, hard asset or personal asset lenders (basically business pawnbrokers) found a niche with small business owners who needed quick cash for special projects or cash flow.

Just like pawning your diamond ring (in fact, depending on the ring, you could find luck using a ring as collateral for a small business loan), these personal asset lenders will take jewelry, luxury cars, and equipment. Unlike traditional pawnbrokers, these lenders claim they cater to a higher-end clientele and offer loans up to $1 million, depending on the collateral.

I recently spoke with a personal asset lender who suggested that this type of financing is a good way for small business owners to fill short-term capital needs.

This new source of money can be obtained from online lenders who will allow you to use your personal luxury assets as collateral. Interest rates are typically 6% per month, so they are too expensive for long-term financing. However, they are proving to be popular with some entrepreneurs who need quick cash to take advantage of a special offer or seize an unexpected opportunity to grow their business.

Some of the items typically used as collateral to secure a short-term, hard-asset loan include:

- Gold and diamond jewelry
- Luxury watches like Rolex, Breitling, and Piaget
- Classic cars like a 1972 Mercedes Benz or even a 1960 Ducati motorcycle

You should also be aware that personal asset lenders expect to hold the collateral as security (like a pawnbroker). So if the lender is not close, they will require you to ship the merchandise to them or they will arrange to hold it in a secure location.

■ **Note** Personal asset lenders charge as much as 6% a month on loans. Be sure you have a short-term need for cash and a solid plan to pay the loan back quickly.

Some of the advantages touted by personal asset lenders include:

- The entire transaction can take place in less than 24 hours
- There are no credit checks or lengthy loan applications
- The personal asset loan allows you to tap into the equity of your luxury assets to secure capital
- You do not need a personal guarantee: your asset fully supports the loan as collateral

This type of financing isn't the best option for everyone, but if you need short-term cash in a hurry, don't have a line of credit, or your credit isn't the best, this is one way to fill the need. Just make sure you have a plan for repaying the loan—6% per month adds up quickly.

Is an Equipment Loan a Good Option for You?

Fueling growth is one of the primary reasons most small business owners turn to the bank for help. I spoke with a small business owner from California not long ago. His business had been steadily growing prior to 2008, but following the financial meltdown, his bank recalled the line of credit he was using to fund his growth.

Even though he had a healthy business and a good credit rating, the tightening of credit by his bank hamstringed his ability to grow. Cash flow kept his business going, but didn't allow for growth. This is not an uncommon scenario on Main Street.

If you need capital equipment to grow your business, an equipment loan might be your best financing option. There can also be tax incentives to financing the equipment you need to do business—including a potential one-time write-off and depreciation throughout the economic life of the equipment.

Equipment loans for specific industries make it relatively simple to acquire the financing you need. There are specialized loans for the following:

- Restaurants
- Construction
- Entertainment
- Dental and medical practices
- Landscaping
- Machine tools
- Technology
- Heavy equipment
- Farm equipment
- Office equipment

Equipment financing or leasing makes it possible for small business owners to purchase the equipment they need, optimize depreciation, and maintain liquidity of other financial resources to manage cash flow.

Note   When you actually purchase certain equipment—like computers, machinery, office furniture, and so on—these purchases can be written off entirely in the current year rather than amortized over time. Talk with your accountant about Section 179 tax deductions (and also *bonus depreciation*) to determine which option makes sense in your situation.

Finding a Lender

Your small business might start with an SBA CDC/504 loan with an affiliated bank and include the other options listed earlier. If the SBA option isn't for you, don't fret that financing provided at the dealership is your only option.

A quick Google search for "equipment loans" returned 109,000,000 results. Many of them include traditional large banks and community banks. Some specialize in farm equipment or medical equipment, for example, but there are a lot of options.

Just like when choosing the right bank, it's important to choose the right partner to help you with your equipment-financing needs. I use the word "partner" intentionally, because although an equipment loan is usually considered an intermediate term loan (it will probably be 15 years or less), you'll still be connected to that lender over the course of the loan. With that in mind, consider these questions when looking for an equipment loan provider:

- Do they understand my industry and the equipment I need to do business?

- Are they local, or will I be working with someone online? (There are some very attractive online options today.)

- If my lender is online, are they available if I have questions?

- Are the loan terms competitive?

- Have I shopped around enough to know that I'm getting the best deal for my situation?

- Do they have any happy customers in my area?

- Do they publish customer testimonials?

- Do I like working with them?

In addition to researching the costs and terms of your equipment purchase, make sure you research the company you're going to finance that purchase with. You should do this regardless of whether you choose to work with a bank, a dealer, or even decide to lease.

Standard Equipment Loan Terms

Approvals are typically based on credit scores, collateral (usually the equipment being financed), financial history, and the market value of the equipment.

- Typical interest rate: 8%–25%

- Typical time to funding: 1–3 months

In addition to providing the loan package described in Chapter 7, be sure to include specifics about the equipment you're purchasing, what you'll be using it for, and how it will improve your ability to increase revenue.

Summary

This chapter described how to secure financing in order to purchase equipment needed for your business. Many small business owners find that equipment financing is a very successful way to acquire the financing they need.

Factoring, covered in Chapter 9, is the chosen finance method for many businesses and has been around for a long time. Although it was once considered a financing option of last resort, factoring is becoming a popular solution for small businesses with short-term capital needs.

Factoring

Tap Into Your Accounts Receivable

Factoring, which involves offering your accounts receivable (AR) to another party at a discount in exchange for immediate cash, has been around for a long time. Its origins lie in international trade and it's said to have started in the ancient world. The Europeans were factoring AR prior to 1400 and the idea came to America with the pilgrims. It's the financial tool that wealthy financiers used to fund shipping companies to make the long voyages to the Orient or the New World to bring back goods like spices, cloth, tobacco, and other precious commodities.

In the truest sense, factoring isn't a loan. The *factor* (the person or company who assumes the liability of the AR) isn't as interested in the credit worthiness of the small business owner as they are in the credit worthiness of the small business' customers. In *non-recourse* factoring, the factor assumes the liability of the AR, but that isn't always the case. In the United States, if the factor doesn't assume the credit risk and is unable to collect, courts will recharacterize the transaction as a secured loan—putting the risk squarely back on the shoulders of the small business owner. Make sure you understand all the terms and fine print before you sign on the dotted line.

There are basically three parties directly involved in a factoring agreement:

- The small business owner who sells the receivable
- The customer of the seller (the account debtor)
- The factor

Many small business owners turn to factoring when their current cash flow doesn't meet their needs, but their AR would be enough if they had immediate access to the funds. Although factoring was traditionally considered an option of last resort, it's become less expensive for the small business owner in recent years. It's grown in popularity as banks and other traditional small business financing options have tightened up the money supply, making traditional financing problematic for small business owners.

There are also some industries, like textiles and apparel, that use factoring because it's the historic method of financing such businesses.

Invoice financing (another name for factoring) is relatively easy to get, although it can be more expensive than traditional financing. Nevertheless, the terms are less restrictive and the funds are available much more quickly—making it an attractive option for many business owners.

▓ **Note**   The terms for factoring are less restrictive than traditional financing, and the cash is available much more swiftly.

Not too long ago I was speaking with a consultant who had landed a fairly substantial contract. Like many small businesses in this situation, the company needed a short-term loan or another line of credit to bridge the gap between the time the contract was initiated and when they would start seeing cash flow from the contract. Unfortunately, they were turned down by all the banks they approached.

Sometimes the problem with securing a large contract is that the company then needs to ramp up employee hiring or buy new equipment to fulfill it. That was the case for this business owner. When the banks said no, the company had to turn to other sources of cash flow to fulfill the contract.

They weren't able to get a short-term loan from the bank, but they were able to factor their AR. They acquired the short-term financing they needed to do business. Although this type of financing isn't for everyone, it does fill a real need for small businesses that banks aren't filling right now.

Is Factoring a Good Choice for Your Situation?

If you use a factor to handle all your accounts receivable, it does come with a cost (usually 2-6% of the invoice). Some factors charge more, which can eat into profit margins pretty quickly. To determine whether factoring is right for you, there are a few questions you need to ask yourself.

Is Your AR Stretched and Causing Cash Flow Problems?

Offering terms to your customers may be a way to increase sales, but net 30-day terms sometimes end up being 40–45 days. If your small business is running on thin margins, things can be painful at the end of the month.

In my own experience, it didn't take long for me to understand that if a customer took over 45 days to pay an invoice, I lost whatever profit I had in that invoice. I didn't turn to factoring, because I was afraid of the costs. Because I didn't really understand factoring at the time and didn't consider the cost of the time I wasted in collections, it hurt my profitability. Not to mention how it diverted me from what was really important—running my business. The 2–6% I would have spent on a factor would probably have been cheaper for me in the long run. My customers always paid me; they just didn't always pay me within 30–45 days.

Do You Miss Out on Opportunities to Grow Because Cash Flow Is Too Tight?

It's been said, "It takes money to make money." That may be true, but it doesn't tell the entire story. For a Main Street business owner, it takes cash flow to seize opportunities and grow. Many small businesses run into cash flow issues when a big order or a new contract opportunity presents itself and cash is tied up in AR.

Earlier in 2013, the National Small Business Association (NSBA) released its 2013 Mid-Year Economic Report.[1] It claimed, "Today, just two-thirds of small businesses (65%) report they are able to obtain adequate financing, down from 73% six months ago."

---

[1]http://www.nsba.biz/wp-content/uploads/2013/08/2013-MY-Report.pdf

When Main Street business owners struggle to find the cash they need to capitalize on a special opportunity through traditional means, they have only a couple of options. They can pass on the new opportunity or look for alternatives. In many cases, factoring is the alternative they're looking for.

Are You Spending a Lot of Time in Collections?

When AR is stretched and cash flow is tight, it's not unusual for small business owners to spend more and more time trying to collect from customers instead of spending the time they need selling to customers. Granted, back-office tasks like collecting are critical to your small business success, but every minute spent doing administrative tasks like collecting from customers is time you can't spend in front of customers solving problems or selling.

Most of us don't start a small business with the idea of being an accountant or collection agent (unless that's your business). Factoring your AR when cash flow is tight helps alleviate these distractions so you can focus on other, maybe more important, parts of your business.

Would Quicker Access to Your Cash Flow Allow You to Take Advantage of Supplier Discounts?

Many suppliers offer discounts to customers who pay their invoices in 10 days or less. You may even be able to negotiate better terms, with the cash in hand, and pay your accounts payable quickly. You may even be able to cancel out the cost of capital—or at least a portion of it.

Are Other Credit Accounts Maxed Out?

Because factoring your AR is not the same thing as a loan or revolving line of credit, your ability to acquire cash is not based on the same criteria. When you're behind the eight ball with cash flow, it doesn't take long to max out credit cards or a line of credit. If your business is doing well and you have a healthy accounts receivable, a factor will allow you to borrow against 80% and sometimes even 90% of your AR. If your AR supports the transaction, the terms are the same whether you're borrowing $5,000, $10,000, $100,000, or even $10,000,000 or more.

The Nuts and Bolts of Factoring

Consider this example of how factoring works, which is pretty simple. Because the textile industry has been using factors to finance the manufacture and distribution of clothing, they provide a pretty straight-forward example. When a clothing manufacturer sells a line of clothing to a department store chain, they deliver the clothes and send an invoice. The factor (sometimes a bank, but many times an alternative lender who specializes in factoring AR) pays the manufacturer a portion of the invoice immediately (typically around 80%, but sometimes more).

Tip Need money fast? A factor, after assessing the creditworthiness of your customers, might give you as much as 80% of the value of your receivables immediately.

The factor then collects the invoice from the department store chain, deducts their fees, and forwards the rest of the invoice to the manufacturer. So if the factor paid you 80% of an invoice of $100,000, the transaction might look like this:

The factor pays 80% of your original invoice ($80,000) now. Once the factor collects the invoice from the customer, they deduct the amount you've already been paid ($100,000 - $80,000 = $20,000) and then deduct their fee (if you are paying 5% to the factor, $100,000 – 5% or $5,000 = $15,000), forwarding to you the additional $15,000.

If you're working with margins greater than 5%, this scenario could be a great option—depending on how much it costs you to collect the money yourself or your need to have quicker access to the lion's share of your invoice.

Factoring Doesn't Carry the Same Stigma It Once Did

There was a time when your customers may have looked down their noses at you for using a factor, but that's not the case these days. Factoring has become a legitimate source of capital for many small business owners since 2008 and the subsequent credit crunch. In fact, many national banks act as factors in some industries and consider it part of their "asset-based commercial lending" portfolio. Banks and other non-bank factors recognize that a small business owner might not be able to afford to wait around for a large company like Walmart to pay an invoice, but they know that Walmart will eventually pay.

What's more, the accounts receivable departments in most companies aren't going to think any less of you if you choose to use a factor. It's become just another part of doing business.

Unlike the bank, a factor is more interested in your future than your credit history. Basically, if a factor is willing to work with you, you can be confident they see money in your future.

A factor can also provide insight into the creditworthiness of your customers. Because they are more interested in your customer's ability to pay their debts, they'll likely do credit research on anyone who owes you money—giving you a valuable look into the creditworthiness of your customers. If the factor isn't interested in purchasing your invoices, it's a possible indication that you might have trouble collecting down the road.

Picking the Right Factor

Just as with any important financial transaction, it's important to know what you're looking for before you sign on the dotted line—particularly when the financial health of your business is concerned. Here are a few questions you should ask a potential factor to help you pick the right one:

- *Do they understand your market?* This sounds like a pretty basic question, but you need someone who understands enough about your market to ensure they can quickly and successfully evaluate the creditworthiness of your customers and approve the highest number of them as possible. If a factor won't work with your customers, he isn't going to do you much good. Some factors are more comfortable in some industries than others; this is something you need to know *before* you choose a factor.

- *What is the cost of the services?* Although there are some pretty standard fees and interest rates, sometimes factoring can feel like buying a used car. The quality and financial stability of your customers can determine your fees and interest rates.

Note Make sure you understand *all* the costs a factor charges. Nobody wants to find out at the last minute about a fee or charge that wasn't discussed. As always, read the fine print.

- *Can you see their references?* Any reputable factor will be more than willing to share references with you—but I wouldn't stop there. Your banker, your accountant, your lawyer, or maybe even one of your friends at the Chamber of Commerce might have a recommendation.

Finding a Reputable Factor

A Google search for "accounts receivable factoring" reveals more than 500,000 results. A good place to start, but I wouldn't stop there. Your tax accountant, attorney, or banker are also good resources. Some factors specialize in particular industries, so you'll want to make sure you find out if they are familiar with your industry, they seem like people you'd want to work with, and have terms you can afford and feel comfortable with. You may also find that the same bank that turned you down for a small business loan is interested in factoring your AR.

Standard Terms for AR Factoring

Although you'll likely pay somewhere in the neighborhood of 2%–6%, don't forget it's a lot like buying a used car—rates are sometimes negotiable depending on the credit health of your customers, the amount receivable on the invoices, and the factor. Make sure you understand all the costs, because they aren't all the same.

Summary

This chapter discussed leveraging your accounts receivable to meet short-term capital needs. The next chapter covers financing designed for purchasing commercial real estate.

Many lenders, including banks and credit unions, will provide a commercial real estate loan to a small business owner whom they would not lend to otherwise. This long-term financing option can be used to purchase new real estate or as collateral for other purposes.

Commercial Real Estate Loans
Location, Location, Location

Many alternative loan products are designed to fill a specific need. Commercial real estate loans are designed to help small business owners finance office buildings, warehouse space, retail shops, industrial buildings, or other stand-alone buildings. Like a home mortgage, this type of loan typically has longer payment terms than the other small business loans you've read about.

Start with the CDC/504

A good place to start a discussion about commercial real estate loans is with the SBA's CDC/504 loan program, introduced in Chapter 5. The short answer to the question of what a 504 loan can be used for is the purchase of land (including existing buildings), improvements (including grading, street improvements, utilities, parking lots, and landscaping), and the construction of new facilities or modernizing, renovating, or converting existing facilities. A borrower cannot use proceeds from a 504 loan for working capital, inventory, consolidating or refinancing debt, or speculative investment in rental real estate.

Unlike many of the other alternative financing options available to small business owners, the 504 loan program provides the same type of long-term, fixed-rate financing enjoyed by larger firms, with interest rates similar to the bond market. (I provide more details about the 504 near the end of the chapter.)

Just as with any other traditional bank loan, your chances of qualifying depend on your credit score, your annual revenues, your ability to repay the loan, and your collateral. Let's take a closer look.

The Three Cs of Commercial Real Estate Lending

An easy way to look at the qualifying process for a real estate loan is to use the *Three Cs*. Your lender will likely be using this or something similar.

Collateral

Prior to 2007, most lenders would regularly approve commercial loans at 75% loan-to-value. Some lenders even went higher than that. Unfortunately, property values plummeted 45 to 50% during the 2008 recession, and these lenders lost a lot of money. Today, the loan-to-value ratios on commercial real estate are closer to 60%. To illustrate the problem, I recently spoke with a borrower who was defaulting on an SBA loan he had secured with roughly $1 million in commercial real estate. Although the loan was collateralized with the real estate, the property lost about 50% of its value—not enough to satisfy the loan. After speaking with his attorney, he got the bad news that he would probably lose his home and all his personal property, which still wouldn't come close to satisfying the debt. The original loan likely had too high a loan-to-value ratio, leaving him and his banker in the lurch. That's not to say you can't get approved at higher than 60%, but you need impeccable credit, strong revenues, and a superior track record in business.

Note If the real estate is occupied, the lender might provide up to 75% of the appraised value. If the real estate is improved but not occupied, you can expect 50%. If the real estate is vacant and unimproved, it will likely be much less.

Cash Flow

One of the primary questions you need to answer is whether your business cash flow can accommodate the monthly obligations associated with the loan. Although there are a number factors that impact the way any particular lender evaluates your business' cash flow numbers, a good starting point is a 1.15:1 ratio of available cash to debt payments. This is not a hard and fast ratio used by every bank.

The most important cash flow question your lender will want answered is whether your business' ongoing sales and collections represent a reliable source of cash that can be used to successfully repay the loan.

Note   A business' cash flow is not limited to the money that goes in and out of a business checking account to operate the business. It also includes any cash flow from investments or other financial activities (payments and receipts or interest and dividends, long-term contracts, insurance, sales, or purchases of machinery, leases, and so on).

Credit Rating

It's been a tough few years for small business owners, particularly those on Main Street. Robbing Peter to pay Paul may keep the doors open this month, but it takes its toll on individual and business credit ratings. Some lenders will accept a lower credit rating than others, but the first thing every lender wants to know is your credit score(s). And yes, if you own a Main Street business, it's likely they'll look at your business score and your personal score.

Additionally, the younger your company is, the more weight they give to your personal credit score. For example, idea-stage startups, and those with only a couple of years in business, can expect the lender to give more weight to personal credit scores. If you have great personal credit, that's not a problem. Conversely, a startup at the idea stage with a founder who has no track record, no income, and bad personal credit is not likely to get a loan.

SIX TIPS TO IMPROVE YOUR CASH FLOW

Here are some ideas for increasing the amount and speed of cash flowing into your business while at the same time limiting the flow outward:

- *Pay off or refinance debt and renegotiate with creditors.* If possible, pay off the debt or refinance the debt for a longer term with lower payments. You may also be able to renegotiate some payment terms with other creditors.

- *Focus on collecting receivables.* I discovered that whatever profit was in a particular invoice was lost if collections went longer than 45 days. What's more, the older the invoices became, the less likely they were to be paid.

- *Give your customers incentives for paying cash.* If you can tighten your credit terms without losing customers, you'll increase the amount of cash on hand. Offer a discount to customers who pay their invoices quickly (within 10 days, for example).

- *Increase revenues.* Although this is certainly easier said than done, poor cash flow is a red flag to lenders (and should be to you) that you need to increase your sales volume.

- *Reduce inventory.* Many businesses utilize a "just in time" inventory strategy to keep their inventory to a minimum. Many suppliers are willing to help you more efficiently manage inventory by supporting your inventory with theirs. Creating an efficient supply chain helps businesses at many levels, including a reduction in your cash flow needs.

- *Review tax strategies that could improve cash flow.* Tax credits are often available for renovating qualified buildings. You may also be able to take advantage of accelerated depreciation on certain equipment and tangible property to increase your short-term tax deductions.

These are just a few ideas for putting your business on a better footing *before* you visit your banker or lender.

Important Questions to Ask Before You Sign on the Dotted Line

If this is your first time seeking a commercial real estate loan, you should know it's not the small business equivalent of a home mortgage. Because commercial lenders are a lot more risk averse, they're likely going to dig into your business financials as well as the commercial property that will be the collateral for the loan. In other words, don't go into this transaction with the same expectations you have for a home mortgage.

Before you apply for the loan, make sure you ask these questions and know the answers:

- *How will you repay the loan?* It's not uncommon for a commercial real estate loan to include a balloon payment at the end of the loan. If you haven't set aside enough savings to pay the balloon payment, you might need to acquire another loan to pay off the balance. This can be problematic if cash flow is poor during the years leading up to the final payment, making it difficult to acquire a loan. You could ultimately risk foreclosure.

  Depending on your industry, if the lender perceives a higher risk in your industry (remember, all lenders are risk averse), he may decide to deny future lending to anyone in your industry—including you.

  There are non-bank, alternative commercial lenders who will make a commercial real estate loan without a balloon payment. Such loans typically incur a point or two higher interest, but work more like a traditional mortgage. It might feel like you're looking into a crystal ball to determine what your business' financial position will be at the end of your loan, but it's something to consider before you close your loan.

- *Can you wait out the loan process?* Most borrowers start by visiting their local bank. A commercial real estate loan from a traditional bank normally includes more stringent requirements and takes the longest time to close when compared to an alternative lender.

  Banks typically go through several phases of review before they approve a loan. They look at your historical income statements, balance sheets, and cash flow. They also want at least the last five years of tax returns of any of the owners who will guarantee the loan.

  You can expect the process to take several weeks before you receive a verbal or written commitment from the bank. Yet, there is still time for the bank's credit committee to veto the loan. If you have great credit and a good relationship with your bank, you might be able to streamline the process, but be aware, the bank is in no rush to process your loan. In other words, the process takes a long time, regardless of your desire to get things accomplished quickly. That's true even if you have solid earnings and a good track record with the bank.

You *are* likely to get the lowest interest rate from a bank. Although non-traditional lenders can respond quicker and might even pre-qualify you in a couple of days, the interest rate will be higher.

• *What types of covenants and conditions are required?* A commercial real estate loan often requires more than simply making timely payments. In addition to monthly payments, some lenders require a quarterly annual income statement, balance sheets, and tax returns on a regular basis over the lifetime of the loan. They may even require a specified debt-to-cash flow ratio, which can become problematic during a downturn.

Even when you make your monthly payments on time, if you don't comply with the other covenants and conditions, your bank might determine you are in default. This triggers a number of penalties, including having to pay back the loan immediately.

This happened to our family business several years ago. My parents purchased a warehouse and were making payments when an industry downturn threatened to impact their business along with a number of their competitors in the area. In a knee-jerk reaction to the bad news, their banker gave them 10 days to pay off their loan or lose the property. Instead of running their business, they had to drop everything and work to find another lender willing to finance their building.

Different lenders require different conditions, so be sure you understand exactly what will be required of you over the course of the loan. In addition to some of the differences already outlined, some alternative lenders will waive any other conditions except for the timely repayment of the loan.

If your financials aren't regularly audited by a CPA firm, you may want to consider an alternative lender and pay the higher interest rate. It might relax the reporting requirements.

- *What type of documents are required?* Most lenders require at least three to five years of financial statements, income tax returns, any current leases, asset statements, relevant corporate documents, and personal tax returns of the business owners. Putting together a loan package similar to the one described in earlier chapters is a great place to start.

  It's always a good idea—before meeting with the lender—to find out what documentation he requires so you can go into the meeting prepared.

- *What happens if you decide to sell the property?* Unlike with a home mortgage, there are usually pre-payment penalties. However, some lenders will allow the new buyer of your property to assume your loan (if they qualify), potentially making it easier to sell the property and get out from under the loan.

- *Are there hidden costs?* In this regard, a commercial real estate loan is a lot like a home mortgage. There are a number of hidden costs you'll need to be aware of. I remember when I purchased my first home, in addition to the interest rate I was quoted, there were fees and charges due at closing that amounted to an extra percent or two. Some of the fees you should watch for include:

  a. Legal fees

  b. Survey charges

  c. Loan application fees

  d. Appraisal charges

  Each of these fees and charges must be either charged against your loan or pre-paid. Depending on the property, some of these charges can amount to tens of thousands of dollars. Because some of these fees must be paid before your loan is approved or rejected, be sure to confer with your banker as to your chances of getting the loan.

  Be sure you know whether the interest rate will change with the prime rate, the bond market, or some other indicator. There are advantages to fixed rates and variable rates, but rates seldom go down.

▓ **Tip** Because the fees and charges can differ when comparing loans and lenders, make sure you ask potential lenders all these questions beforehand so you can make an informed decision.

Is a Commercial Real Estate Loan a Good Idea for Your Small Business?

There are a number of reasons a commercial real estate loan could be a good idea for your business.

A Real Estate-Secured Line of Credit

Many banks allow small business owners to establish a line of credit secured against the real estate the business owns. This can enable the business owner to leverage the equity in their property for a higher line of credit than might otherwise be available.

A Real Estate-Secured Loan

Although the SBA CDC/504 loan program doesn't allow you to use the proceeds for other purposes, there are other lenders who will allow you to use the equity of your business property for other purposes, including working capital, inventory, and consolidating or refinancing debt.

A Real Estate-Secured Loan to Refinance an Existing Commercial Mortgage

Business owners who want to take advantage of a lower interest rate or better covenants or conditions might opt to refinance their current real estate loan.

A Real Estate-Secured Loan for the Purpose of Purchasing Commercial Property

This is the primary intent of the SBA's 504 loan program. These loans are designed to enable small business owners to purchase property to conduct business. What's more, if this is the reason you are seeking a commercial real estate loan, the 504 program is a great option. The SBA CDC/504 loan program has many advantages, including:

- *Unlike most commercial real estate loans, a 504 loan is designed to finance the total project cost.* That includes existing structures, construction/renovation costs, furniture, fixtures, and equipment. The ability to roll these costs into the loan instead of pre-paying them can be beneficial to Main Street business owners.

- *504 loans have lower equity requirements than conventional commercial financing options.* This keeps less of the borrower's capital tied up and more of it available for running the business.

- *The 504 loan terms are often more attractive.* The rates are usually below market. For example, in 2013, they were between 4.2 and 5.2%.

Where Should You Look for a Loan?

Banks, credit unions, brokers, and a number of alternative lenders offer commercial real estate loans. Depending on your credit rating, the nature of the loan, and other factors listed in this chapter, you can make a choice.

If you're not sure where to start, a quick search on Google will introduce you to over 30 million potential lenders. If you want to narrow it down from there, commercial real estate brokers can recommend their favorite lenders. Additionally, your attorney or CPA can probably make recommendations.

Standard Terms for Commercial Real Estate Loans

Other than the terms already discussed in this chapter, most commercial lenders will offer loan terms up to 10 years with a balloon payment or up to 15 years with full amortization. Interest rates are difficult to quote as they fluctuate so much, but expect to pay around 0.5% of the amount financed up front (it could be more or less, depending on the lender).

Summary

Commercial real estate loans can help business owners acquire long-term financing to purchase property or help them leverage the equity in currently owned property to obtain capital. The next chapter discusses the merchant cash advance, which is a distant cousin of factoring.

Like factoring, which leverages a small business' accounts receivables, a merchant cash advance leverages a small business' regular and predictable credit card transactions to access capital for short-term capital needs.

The Merchant Cash Advance

Credit or Debit?

Young businesses, even thriving ones, often struggle to find the cash they need to grow and operate. If they've been in business less than five years, they don't have a track record. If they've been operating on a shoestring, they probably don't have the best credit rating. I know several young entrepreneurs who used their personal credit cards to keep the doors open—which can sometimes be problematic from a credit-management perspective.

A merchant cash advance (MCA) isn't really a loan. It is an advance based on the volume of cash that flows through a company's merchant cash account—in other words, the monthly flow of credit card transactions you have each month. A regular, predictable flow of credit card transactions can be all a young and thriving company needs to secure financing for working capital or expansion, even when they don't have a 720 credit score or a big wad of cash in the bank.

■ **Note**   Although it's not technically a loan, a merchant cash advance is often referred to as an MCA loan by those who offer this type of financing.

That doesn't mean MCA lenders don't look at your credit rating. They do. In fact, just as with any other loan, the lender will ask you about your credit rating, time in business, monthly revenues, and so on. They just happen to rate the number and amount of your credit card transactions as more relevant.

Where Did MCAs Come From?

AdvanceMe, then based out of Kennesaw, Georgia, was the first (and only) such lender a decade or so ago. Since that time, dozens more have entered the market, which has bloomed from less than $10 million to well over half a billion dollars a year. Because capital has been so difficult for Main Street businesses to acquire in recent years, MCA lenders are aggressively looking for (and finding) borrowers who meet the right profile.

Although it's not uncommon to hear this type of financing referred to as a "business payday loan," it all depends on the particular lender and how *you* approach the transaction. Traditional lenders like banks and credit unions are regulated by a number of state and federal agencies, while MCA lenders don't face that same scrutiny. That means it's very important to spend the time to investigate the lenders before you make your decision. I don't recommend going with the first MCA lender you come across; be sure to speak to three or so first.

When I was a young entrepreneur, I wasn't aware of this type of financing. However, I remember what it's like to need cash quickly. Despite how much you might need the financing, don't leap into a relationship before you look.

If a lender offers you a lot more money than you are asking for and isn't very concerned about your ability to repay the advance, this should raise many red flags. That being said, there are a number of great MCA lenders worthy of consideration. My advice is to treat looking for an MCA lender the same way you treat buying a used car—do the research and be prepared to walk away from a deal that just doesn't seem right.

Qualifying for a Merchant Cash Advance

An MCA is similar to accounts receivable factoring (covered in Chapter 9). It isn't for everyone. Like factoring, it's anywhere from a little more expensive to a lot more expensive than a traditional term loan. Nevertheless, there are situations when tapping into your credit card transactions makes sense for you and your business.

The terms and requirements for an MCA are a lot less stringent than a traditional loan, and there are other requirements an MCA lender will consider in addition to your credit score, time in business, and annual revenue. Like some of the other alternative financing sources you've read about, most MCA lenders are non-bank lenders. You'll want to investigate and compare a few before you settle in and make a choice. Although they are looking for similar things, there might be some variation, so consider the following items as a starting place for comparison rather than hard-and-fast rules.

- *You need to maintain at least $2,500 to $5,000 in monthly credit card transactions.* Although every lender is different, this is a good range to consider before you go to an MCA lender. You should also be aware that an MCA lender will debit your payment directly from your merchant cash account—this makes your credit rating less important if you have the monthly transactions to support their terms. Because they won't be waiting for you to make a payment and have access to your merchant account, they're more confident they'll get paid. And, unlike the bank that wants to see a track record of four years or longer, you'll likely qualify if you've been in business for around a year.

- *You can't already be working with another MCA lender.* This shouldn't be a surprise to anyone. Although it's possible to have a couple of small business loans or lines of credit open simultaneously, if you already have a merchant cash advance in place, you can't get another one until the current advance is paid off.

- *There can't be current liens on business-owned property.* This is another stipulation that should make sense. Although the risk tolerance of an MCA lender is different than that of a banker, like any other loan, there are red flags that will kill the deal.

- *You need to provide financial data to validate sales and monthly credit card receipts.* An MCA lender may be less interested in your credit score than your banker, but they are very interested in your merchant account. They'll want to see your merchant account statements for several months to validate that you have enough transaction volume to support the advance.

Like a factor, an MCA lender will be looking at your future receipts as collateral. Some lenders want to know how the loan will be used (which makes sense) and others will work only with businesses that have been around for a year or more. You should also remember that an MCA is more expensive than other traditional financing. However, if you don't qualify for a term loan or line of credit at the bank, this could be a viable option.

Another benefit of an MCA is time to funding. I recently spoke with a banker who stated that he doesn't even look at an application for an SBA 7(a) loan for six weeks. He suggested the typical time to funding was six months or more. In many cases, a merchant cash advance is approved in hours and even funded in hours or days. So if you need cash right away, an MCA can be a viable option.

What Types of Businesses Are Good Matches for a Merchant Cash Advance?

Fortunately, some of the businesses that typically struggle to find traditional financing are exactly what MCA lenders are looking for. An MCA is often a good match for:

- Service businesses

- Restaurants

- Retail businesses

Just about any business that does a lot of credit card transactions is a good candidate for an MCA. Some MCA lenders will advance up to $500,000—depending on your Visa/MasterCard volume over the last 90 to 120 days. A good rule of thumb is that you can receive about 125% of your monthly transaction volume averaged over the previous 120 days.

Note   Restaurants and retail business that regularly take credit cards are often a good match for an MCA.

How Do You Determine Which MCA Lender Is Right for You?

Like most alternative lenders, MCA lenders come in all shapes and sizes. You want to make sure the lender you choose is right for your situation. Fortunately, this is a very popular vehicle for acquiring funds and, as more of these lenders enter the market, the costs are becoming more reasonable. Nevertheless, I doubt the rates they charge will ever favorably compete with a traditional term loan.

Here are a few things you'll want to make sure you have a handle on *before* you sign on the dotted line:

- *Make sure you understand all the fees upfront.* Don't assume that because you understand the fees at one MCA lender you understand them all. I've spoken to more than one borrower who was surprised by an unexpected fee. If you have a lender who refuses to explain everything before you sign, it's time to start looking for another lender. Don't settle for a bad deal; there are a number of very reputable MCA lenders who are willing to explain how they work—including explaining all the fees they charge.

- *Make sure you understand the terms.* Depending on the lender, some advances involve a daily fixed amount taken from your account while others take a percentage of your credit card sales each day. One lender might take 10% of your transactions every day until you've paid back the entire advance, whereas others might take a fixed amount, such as $100. If your lender takes 10% every day, don't confuse that with the interest rate—sometimes they can be substantially higher.

  I recently spoke to one borrower who expected to have his loan paid off in 90 days. He didn't notice in the fine print that if it wasn't paid off in that time, the lender would take all of the cash in his merchant account until he had paid the balance in full. He was using his MCA as a short-term solution to take advantage of a unique opportunity to pre-sell some special merchandise, but he neglected to account for the extra month required to collect from his customers. When he didn't pay the balance of his MCA off within the agreed-upon 90 days, his lender did just as stipulated within the contract and proceeded to drain his merchant account each day. This was not only an unwelcome surprise; it caused serious cash flow issues for his business.

- *Make sure your lender gives you at least an estimate of a projected annual percentage rate (APR).* Although there are a number of advantages to an MCA, a low interest rate doesn't happen to be one of them. This will make it much easier to avoid comparing apples and oranges when comparing MCA lenders. There are definitely lower-cost alternatives to an MCA if you qualify for them.

- *Don't use the first MCA lender willing to work with you.* Over the last couple of years there have been a number of new lenders enter the market, pushing rates and fees down, and making it more attractive for small business owners. Make sure you've shopped several lenders before you decide. The differences between lenders can be surprising. Shopping around is the only way to ensure you get the best possible rates and the lowest fees.

Tip   Shop around to get the best MCA rate and read that fine print carefully. You're probably eager for the advance and may let your guard down as a result. Don't. You can make a mistake that has the potential to put you out of business.

If your merchant cash advance is like most, the lender deducts a percentage of your credit card transactions until the balance is paid—this makes it easier for you to get through a cash flow crunch if business slows down for some reason. When times are good, the advance is paid off quicker, and when times are tight, they take less.

It's true, an MCA is a higher-cost alternative to a loan from the bank, but the duration of this type of financing is typically short term and, when used wisely, it can be a powerful financial tool for small business owners. In fact, many borrowers use an advance as a bridge to a larger term loan because the time to funding is so short.

Three of the biggest advantages of a merchant cash advance are:

- *It's quick and relatively easy to qualify.* Unlike with a term loan, you can get the cash you're looking for in 72 hours or less. Some lenders can underwrite and approve your advance in less than 24 hours. If you need cash to address an immediate need, this could be a good option for you.

- *Quick access to additional cash can enable you to take advantage of opportunities.* Many small business owners will use an advance to leverage short-term opportunities into long-term expansion.

- *There are fewer restrictions on how you can use the advance.* Unlike with an SBA loan or other traditional loan, once you have the cash there are fewer restrictions on how you can use it.

A couple things to watch out for when considering an MCA:

- *Pay attention to the interest rate.* Some MCA lenders charge up to 20 or 30%, or even more. A merchant cash advance can be a great short-term solution to a cash flow problem, a way to take advantage of a special offer from a supplier, or even a bridge to a traditional term loan. When any particular advance becomes a long-term solution to a need for cash, they get expensive—very expensive. Over time, it becomes less about the monthly obligation and more about the cost of capital.

- *Even though you didn't put any collateral at risk, beware.* Although you might not be required to put up any collateral to obtain an MCA the same way a young entrepreneur might second-mortgage his home at the bank, your home could still be at risk. It's true that if your business fails, you have no legal obligation to repay the advance. That is, unless you don't strictly follow the terms of the contract. For example, you can't encourage your customers to pay in cash or switch credit card processors. If an MCA lender suspects that you have broken the terms of the contract, they may aggressively pursue you for repayment—including going after personal assets.

Despite some of the folklore surrounding merchant cash advances, it's not the harbinger of financial ruin that some think it is. Over the last couple of years, even as credit restrictions have relaxed for "bigger" small business owners, the smallest small businesses are still struggling to find cash. More and more business owners are successfully turning to products like the merchant cash advance to find the funding they need.

▓ **Tip**   An MCA—arranged with eyes wide open—can be a good way to bridge a short bout of poor cash flow. But don't let it become a vehicle for long-term financing. That's a situation bound to end in tears.

Where Should You Look for a Merchant Cash Advance?

Most MCA lenders have a strong presence online, so start with search on Google. When I searched for "Merchant Cash Advance Companies," I got over 4 million hits. If you know a business owner who has used this type of financing, a personal recommendation goes a long way. If you reach out to any particular lender, ask for references who you can call and speak with about their experience. Don't be content with the testimonials on their website.

Standard Terms for a Merchant Cash Advance

Although there are no industry standards, it's not uncommon for an MCA lender to advance up to 125% of monthly credit card sales. Most advances are for terms of six to ten months. Expect the lender to take 5–10% (or more, depending on the lender) of every credit card and/or debit card transaction every month until the balance is paid. Although 5–10% might not sound like much, remember it's 5–10% *per month*, making the annual percentage rate quite high. This is not a long-term solution.

Summary

A merchant cash advance is one of the more popular alternative methods of financing short-term capital needs today. Because there are so many MCA lenders (terms and conditions vary), make sure to speak to more than one lender to compare terms and ensure you have the right loan for your business.

As described in this chapter, the wise use of an MCA can be an excellent source of capital. Just as with a business credit card, which is the topic of the following chapter, it's important to make sure you completely understand the fine print and use the resource intelligently.

They Call It a Credit Card for a Reason

Don't Leave Home Without It

I couldn't help but think of the actor Karl Malden when I got my first credit card. I remember him as kind of a hard-nose cop on the TV show, *The Streets of San Francisco.*[1] His co-star was a very young Michael Douglas. I remember watching the show as a teenager. Malden had enough street cred from the series; I can still remember an American Express ad that featured him as their spokesperson. Although Malden was talking about Travelers Checks when he said, "Don't leave home without them," the tag line eventually applied to the American Express card too.

A business credit card is probably the easiest entry into establishing credit at a traditional small business lender like a bank or credit union. And, as mentioned, I've known quite a few young entrepreneurs who have used credit cards to finance operations in the early years. But I wouldn't recommend it. Early in my career, I worked for someone who had a dozen credit cards in his wallet and used them to purchase supplies, fund projects, and augment cash flow. He was one of the most disciplined people

[1] http://www.imdb.com/title/tt0068135/

I've ever met. He seldom let anything go over 30 days and rarely carried a balance. He paid very little interest, but using credit cards in this way, for most people, can be much like walking a knife's edge—one slip can spell disaster.

That's not to say a business credit card isn't a valuable tool when used appropriately.

Why Would You Want a Business Credit Card?

The National Small Business Association (NSBA) reports[2] that 31% of the small businesses they surveyed had used a credit card in the previous 12 months to finance a business need. In fact, it shouldn't be a surprise that credit cards are at the top of the list for most Main Street business owners who need quick cash. Many businesses, like the disciplined friend I described previously, are likely to use a combination of business and personal credit cards, but a business-specific card has its advantages.

Tip   One of the first things my accountant told me was to keep my personal finances and my business finances separate. This is much easier said than done, especially when you're using the same credit card to buy a necessary piece of equipment for the office that you use to take your family to Disneyland. A business credit card makes it much easier for your accountant, and the IRS, to tell the difference between personal and business expenditures.

Here are a few of the benefits a business credit card provides:

- *Keeps track of employee expenditures and serves as an audit trail.* Most of the Main Street business owners I know don't give credit cards to their employees willy-nilly, but there are scenarios where it makes a lot of sense. Along with the ability to monitor monthly statements and balance expense accounts with those statements, some business credit cards even allow you to set limits on the amount employees can spend.

---

[2]http://www.nsba.biz/wp-content/uploads/2013/02/2012-Year-End-Economic-Report-Final.pdf

I also know credit card providers who promote business credit cards as a way to reduce the cost of writing a purchase order for smaller business purchases. Instead of creating a P.O. for purchases of less than $100 or $200 (depending upon what you believe is a smaller purchase), buyers are authorized to use the credit card to make the purchase. The statement from the credit card company acts as an audit trail.

- *Offers higher spending limits.* Some business credit cards offer limits far greater than a typical Gold or Platinum card and some larger banks give business owners access to well over a hundred additional cards (for employees).

- *Can offer attractive rewards programs.* Not unlike your personal credit card, many business credit cards offer incentives to use their card. Depending on the card, they offer cash back, discounts on office supplies, travel benefits, and discounts on other business services.

- *Provides terms designed for businesses.* As a business owner, you might not be able to pay the balance at the end of the month. Some card providers, like American Express, offer discounts for those who pay their balance early or up to 60 days without interest (the Plum card offers this benefit). Sixty days without interest can be a great way to meet a short-term cash flow need.

 Tip Use your card to improve your business credit. If you're running a startup or are an early stage entrepreneur, most lenders will look at your personal credit score to determine if you're a good credit risk. In much the same way that you've used credit to build your personal credit score, a business credit card can build business credit. (And, yes, you need to pay attention to your business credit score as well as your personal credit score.)

Personal Credit Cards and Business Credit Cards Are *Not* the Same

There are certainly advantages to a business credit card, but there are also some disadvantages that you can't ignore. Many of the consumer protections that have been legislated over the years for consumer credit cards don't apply to business credit cards. I learned about one of them the hard way.

Like most Main Street startups at the time, my access to credit included a second mortgage on my house and a couple of business credit cards. My business lived or died on the cash flow we generated doing our day-to-day sales. I used the cards to buy equipment and pay for any business-related supplies we needed. For the most part, I kept on top of my monthly obligations, but there were times when I would rob Peter to pay Paul. One month I had a small balance on one of the cards. I think it was a couple hundred dollars. Because the amount was relatively insignificant, I put off paying the card balance that week. The low interest rate they originally offered on the card shot through the roof—basically making the card far too expensive to use. Because I wasn't paying attention to the small print, I was also hit with a fee or two that I wasn't too excited about paying. Although I didn't (and still don't) agree with that practice, it was my lack of attention to the fine print, and stupidity, that cost me.

Note   In an earlier chapter, I mentioned how the "mouse type" is so small that only a mouse can read it. Card providers make it difficult to read so you will skip over it. Don't make that mistake. Make sure you read and understand it before you get the card.

The following sections outline a few other differences between personal and business credit cards.

You Aren't Protected from Arbitrary-Feeling/ Surprise Rate Increases

The CARD Act[3] protects the average consumer from what can feel like an arbitrary-feeling rate increase by requiring a 45-day notice before increases take effect. This isn't the case for business credit cards.

Not only can business credit card lenders raise the interest rate any time they want, they can also apply those interest rates to any older charges—something they can't do on a consumer credit card.

Some credit cards comply with the CARD Act even on business credit cards, which I think they should. Others retroactively apply new interest rates to old purchases, but give their cardholders the 45-day notice. Make sure you understand what happens when your bank or credit card provider raises their interest rates—because it will eventually happen.

---

[3]The Credit Card Accountability, Responsibility, and Disclosure Act

Don't Expect to Have 30 Days to Pay Your Credit Card Bill

The CARD Act requires that lenders mail the credit card statement to consumers at least 21 days before the bill is due. This doesn't apply to business credit cards and, what's more, payment doesn't have to fall on the same day each month. You need to pay attention to when your credit card bill is due and make timely payments—it's up to you to know if the due dates are on different days.

Some credit card providers do give their business card holders at least 21 days and have the same due date every month for payment, even though it's not required by the CARD Act. This is another reason to shop around for your business credit card provider.

Caps on Late Fees? Fugedaboudit

Although the CARD Act caps late fees for consumer cards at $25 or the minimum payment, business credit card late fees are not regulated. Fees can add up pretty quickly.

There isn't a limit on over-limit fees, either. Many business card issuers automatically let you go over your limit and in some cases the over-limit fees can amount to more than your charges. Personal credit card holders must opt in to over-limit fees.

You've already read about some of the benefits of a business credit card over a personal credit card, but it's not all peaches and cream. Make sure you understand all the terms and conditions before you take the new card. If the business card offer came to you in the mail, look for, read, and understand all the disclaimers before you apply. If you're going to the local bank, make sure you take the time to go through that same document with someone at the bank who can explain everything to you in simple-to-understand language.

How to Avoid Credit Card Surprises

Earlier in this chapter I suggested it was my laziness or stupidity that caught me holding the bag for a jump in interest rate and fees I wasn't expecting. My cavalier attitude forced me to pay additional fees that I shouldn't have. With a little bit of diligence on my part, I could have avoided the surprise. I took for granted that the same rules applied to my personal credit card as my business card. There are some other things you should know that will help you avoid a surprise or two yourself.

- *Make sure you understand the gobbledygook.* Every industry has its own acronyms and vocabulary. Credit cards have a unique vocabulary too. Learning the unique language of credit cards will help you avoid surprise charges and fees.

  - **APR (annual percentage rate):** As you might expect, this is the interest rate you pay annually on any unpaid balance you carry on your card. In other words, this is the interest rate you pay if you don't pay the balance on the due date.

  - **Promotional or introductory:** The "introductory" interest rate on a new credit card may be very low, but it's only temporary. This is a marketing tactic used by credit card providers to entice you to sign up for their credit card. Those rates are temporary and the rate will go up after the promotional period is over. If you sign up for a credit card with a promotional rate, it's important that you know how long the rate will last so you don't get surprised with an unexpected rate increase.

  - **Grace period:** This is a very important term and describes the time you have to pay your credit card bill without incurring interest. On consumer credit cards, the grace period is required to be at least 21 days and some providers even allow 30 days. Don't automatically expect it to be the same with business credit card providers. Make sure you ask.

- *Break out the magnifying glass.* Some content is written to be read and understood, but most of the time that isn't true of the small print on the back of your credit card application. Although the fine print might be a lot easier to understand than it once was, brace yourself. The text is small, it's not in a very readable typeface, and there's a lot of it. But don't quit because it's tough; you need to understand all of it.

  Make a list of all the terms you don't understand so you can look them up or ask what they mean. Assuming you're okay with something you're not 100% sure about could cost you through surprise fees or a jump in interest rate down the road.

- *Don't be afraid you're going to ask a dumb question.* Once you've read the agreement and have your list of questions, talk to the card provider. Visit your bank branch or call the customer service line and go through *all* the questions you have. Ask them to explain what is unclear, and if it's still unclear, ask again.

  If they aren't willing to explain their terms, it's time to find another lender. Period. If this is how they treat you before you've signed on the dotted line, imagine how they are going to treat you once you owe them money.

- *Google the provider.* Believe me when I tell you, if there's anything negative about your potential business credit card provider, you'll probably find it online. Every provider, even the good ones, have disgruntled folks bashing them online. If there are more than a few complaints, it should throw up a red flag.

  Treat negative online reviews the same way you do the purchase of anything else online. Read them, balance them against the good reviews, and make a decision. Whenever I read reviews, I automatically eliminate the most positive and most negative review (there are always outliers). I try to look at the folks in the middle of the curve. Keep in mind that unhappy customers are more likely to publish reviews than satisfied ones. Take that into consideration.

Paying attention and following these simple suggestions won't guarantee that you'll never get a surprise charge or fee, but they will definitely help. I wish I had been aware and paid more attention to these four suggestions.

Walking the Razor's Edge

Earlier in this chapter I mentioned my friend who used several different credit cards to finance his business operations. Although there are success stories out there, I thought I'd share a few reasons why I think this is a horrible idea:

- *Many of these stories are exaggerated.* Even if their credit cards were the only real source of credit they had early in their business, it's more likely they survived on good old cash flow, not their credit card balance. Years ago, two friends who were also professional colleagues would joke about how you could only believe 43% of what the other said. Sadly, over the years I found that to be true about one of them. He really liked to embellish the facts when he described how he started his business.

- *I wish I had a nickel for every time I've heard the story of a successful company launched on the back of maxed-out credit cards.* I've been there. And yes, aside from my second mortgage, credit cards were the only type of credit I had. I used those credit cards to finance special purchases that *I couldn't make any other way.* Credit cards are a pretty expensive (although convenient) way to finance purchases, and just aren't practical as a sole means of financing your business. You don't hear about the companies who failed when they bet everything on the idea they could pay off the credit cards just before the lenders lowered the boom.

- *Most people, myself included, just aren't disciplined enough.* It's far too easy, and likely a part of human nature, to pay the minimum balance every time the statement is due. The only reason it worked for my friend is because he had the discipline to pay the balance off when the statement arrived every month. If you don't have that type of discipline, it doesn't take long for your business credit card balance to spiral out of control. Once that happens, and once you carry a significant unpaid balance each month, it makes it more difficult if not impossible to acquire other forms of financing when you really need them.

Finding the Right Business Credit Card

Although your local bank or credit union usually offers a business credit card, don't feel like that is your only option. It is convenient to sit across the desk from someone you already know to ask questions and make sure you understand the terms, but there are other credit card providers who specialize in business credit cards.

Your accountant or CPA might also be able to offer some insight into good credit card providers. Just as with the other financing sources you've read about, the Internet is a great place to look. I Googled "business credit card providers" and got over 51 million results. Needless to say, you have a lot of options.

Standard Terms for a Business Credit Card

Bankrate.com[4] reports that, as of September 2013, the average APR for variable-rate credit cards is 15.36%. It's not uncommon for this rate to change over the course of a year. The rate on a fixed-rate card is 13.02%.

Tip Business credit cards are good for buying almost anything your business needs, provided you pay off the bill every month to avoid interest charges. That said, it sometimes makes sense to pay the interest fee when you absolutely need something important to generate revenue and can't secure a conventional business loan.

Summary

This chapter explained some of the differences between a personal and business credit card and discussed why a small business owner might choose to use a business card. As with any line of credit, the wise use of a business credit card not only provides capital to fill a quick and short-term need, it provides an opportunity for early-stage business owners to build their business credit rating and demonstrate their credit-worthiness.

The next chapter discusses peer-to-peer lending and what are commonly called "3F" loans.

---

[4]http://www.bankrate.com/finance/credit-cards/rate-roundup.aspx

Peer-to-Peer Loans

Brother, Can You Spare a Dime?

One of the toughest stages for an entrepreneur to find financing is during the startup phase. It's even tougher if your startup is in the idea stage, has no revenues, and doesn't even have a real product yet.

Although I'm not a regular viewer, I enjoy the occasional episode of the ABC TV show, *Shark Tank*.[1] In one show, a pair of entrepreneurs excitedly pitched what they believed was a slam dunk (if only one or more of the sharks would join them). They had a working prototype, they had researched the market, and they had a fairly compelling pitch. What they didn't have was a track record, any revenue, or any distribution. They couldn't understand why none of the sharks were interested.

The investors on *Shark Tank* are angel investors. In a lot of ways, angels act a lot like what are known as peer-to-peer lenders (although they do want some equity in the venture). Peer-to-peer lending bypasses the bank and puts borrowers in front of individuals with money to lend. Unlike the angels on *Shark Tank*, however, most peer-to-peer lenders are average folks whose investment is combined with the money other investors just like them put in the project. Although there are a number of web sites that match potential peer-to-peer lenders with borrowers, getting a loan from your rich uncle Fred can also be considered a peer-to-peer loan.

---

[1]http://abc.go.com/shows/shark-tank

Lending Club[2] is a great example of how a peer-to-peer lending organization works:

1. Borrowers apply for loans, and investors on the network invest.

2. Borrowers get funded and investors create a portfolio of investments.

3. Borrowers repay the loan and investors earn interest and reinvest.

Most peer-to-peer loans are unsecured personal loans. Unlike traditional loans, and many alternative loans, the transaction is between individuals and not companies. Interest rates are determined by the individual investor, but like other lenders, the interest rates are determined based upon the lender's risk tolerance and the perception of how risky a loan to any particular borrower might be.

On most peer-to-peer web sites, lenders compete for borrowers and the lowest rate using a reverse auction model. In other words, the rolls of the buyer and seller are reversed. The seller, in this case the lender, competes with other lenders to woo individual borrowers.

When I first entered the workforce, I participated in many reverse auctions in an effort to secure government contracts for the company I was working for at the time. Although we didn't call it a reverse auction, the bidding process is a good example. The procurement officer would make a request for bid, and if our price was the lowest price to honor the terms of the contract, we won the bid. Unlike a traditional auction similar to those conducted on eBay,[3] where many buyers bid on a single item, there are some peer-to-peer lending sites that use the reverse auction model. Imagine an eBay auction where sellers bid against each other to sell you their item at the lowest possible price.

---

[2]https://www.lendingclub.com/public/how-peer-lending-works.action
[3]http://www.ebay.com

Peer-to-Peer Lending vs. Traditional Lending

In many respects, the main difference between peer-to-peer lending and traditional lending lies in the parties involved. Like most traditional or alternative loans, a peer-to-peer loan is made to create a profit. However, there are differences you'll want to be aware of as you consider this type of funding:

- It is unlikely there will be a prior connection between the borrower or the lender.

- The transaction usually takes place online and is intermediated by a peer-to-peer lending company.

- Individual investors choose which borrowers they will invest in.

- The loans are unsecured and are not protected by any government insurance.

- The loans are treated as securities that may be sold to other investors.

The History of Peer-to-Peer Lending

Although in its most basic form peer-to-peer lending has been going on since ancient times, I limit this conversation to the modern version. The Internet has given peer-to-peer lending a set of legs, making it possible for borrowers from all over the world to connect with individual investors. Today, peer-to-peer lending takes place in the United States and Great Britain, and is also gaining popularity in the Far East.

Social networks are also a big part of the phenomenon, because they enable borrowers and investors to connect via social media. The emergence of peer-to-peer lending is likely a reaction to the need for options normally unavailable at the local bank.

Imperfect Credit?

Most Main Street business owners don't turn to peer-to-peer lenders if they can walk into the bank with an application and leave with a loan. Like the other types of funding discussed in this book, peer-to-peer loans are an option for small business owners who have been forced to make some pretty tough decisions over the last few years and have less than perfect credit. Nevertheless, that doesn't mean you must have sketchy credit to participate; some borrowers and lenders choose peer-to-peer lending for philosophical reasons. Here are some other reasons why a peer-to-peer loan might be a good option:

- *Peer-to-peer lenders often look at more than your credit score.* Most peer-to-peer lending companies utilize the Internet to collect a more complete profile of the potential borrower. Although credit score is an important metric, it's only one measure of a business' viability. Because they also have access to the profiles of thousands of previous loans (many just like yours), investor networks have a lot of data with which to compare and make decisions about any small business, including yours.

- *Reasonable interest rates.* Although the interest rates are higher than with a traditional loan, they are more favorable than some of the other alternative financing options. Depending on how high the risk for your loan is rated, you can expect to pay between 7–8% or even as much as 30%. Much depends on your credit rating, the health of your business, and the loan amount you're looking for.

- *Peer-to-peer loans are sized right for Main Street businesses.* Most peer-to-peer loans would be considered micro loans by the SBA, because the maximum loan amount is closer $35,000, rather than $350,000.

- *Quick access to cash.* It's not uncommon to wait six weeks before you're even able to talk to anyone about an SBA loan, and likely months before your loan would be funded. With peer-to-peer loans, everything is done online. Therefore, many people who apply for a loan have the money deposited in their bank account within 10 days.

- *No penalty for prepayment.* Although peer-to-peer lenders lose a little interest when a borrower pays off their balance early, there are no penalties. Prepayment fees at a bank can get expensive, but that's not something you need to worry about with a peer-to-peer lender.

- *Real people, not institutions, do the lending.* Community banks talk a lot about community lending, but this is grassroots community lending unlike anything a bank can provide.

Successfully Finding Peer-to-Peer Funding

Although it might sound pretty simple to log in to a peer-to-peer funding site, fill out a profile, and watch the money roll in, don't be deceived. There are a lot of small business owners who never get the funding they need on these sites. Here are a few suggestions that might improve your odds:

- *Don't be greedy.* Although peer-to-peer lending isn't the same as going into a bank, most of these folks are pretty savvy lenders. If you've been turned down by the local bank because your credit score was too low, don't expect these folks to ignore your credit score. They may be more risk tolerant than the bank (which is one reason you pay a higher interest rate), but they're not anxious to throw their money away. It might be wise to be conservative about the amount you ask for.

- *Location, location, location.* Make sure you take some time to research the right peer-to-peer lending site to work with. Some sites are geared more toward start-ups whereas others are for specific industries—make sure you're making your pitch in the right place.

- *Don't make people guess.* Make sure you explain what you need the funding for. If you plan on updating your web site, redesigning packaging, or ramping up your marketing, spell it out. These investors want to know as much about who you are and what you're going to do with the financing as they can to make an informed decision.

- *The devil is in the details.* Not only do these lenders want to know what you're going to do with the cash, they want to know about you and your company. The more information you share (including an explanation about why you might have a poor credit score), the more likely you'll get the financing you need.

▓ **Tip**   With the exception of borrowing from friends and family, peer-to-peer lending is usually done online. A search for "peer-to-peer lending companies" reveals lots of information about peer-to-peer lending in general, but also identifies a number of lenders.

Caveat Emptor: Let the Borrower Beware

Although peer-to-peer lending might be just the right option for your small business, there are some potential pitfalls you should be aware of. Although many of these lending companies have been around for a few years now and many small business owners just like you are getting funding this way, this type of funding isn't for everyone.

- *You might not get what you're asking for.* Most of the time, a peer-to-peer loan is an aggregate of several individuals whose funds are pooled to finance your requested loan amount. Say you take the time to create a pitch, spend the effort you'll need to promote the purpose of your loan, and make a case successfully. If there aren't enough individuals willing to invest in your cause, you might fall short of your goal.

- *Peer-to-peer loans aren't regulated by any government agency.* Because individuals are the lenders and the Internet is the connection between the lenders and the borrowers, funds can come from anywhere in the country (or around the world, for that matter). Make sure you read all the documentation on the site before you jump in with both feet.

- *You'll likely pay a higher interest rate.* As you might expect, you'll probably pay a higher interest rate for a peer-to-peer loan. You've read about some of the advantages of a peer-to-peer loan, so if you can stand the idea of a higher interest rate, this type of loan could be a good fit for you.

A Borrower's Success Story

Because I've had no personal experience with any borrowers who've turned to peer-to-peer lending to financing, I decided to go to one of the biggest peer-to-peer lenders (Prosper) to see if they had any stories to share. Yes, they did.

After six years, a young fashion designer needed some funds to keep up with demand and expand her business (sound familiar?). She borrowed from family and friends along with tapping her personal credit cards. Just like many small business owners, she didn't have the credit history or collateral needed to get a bank loan.

At the advice of a friend, she visited Prosper's site, created a listing, and almost immediately had eight investors interested in her loan. Like many of the small business owners I talk to, it doesn't always take a lot to keep the small business engine running. Her first loan was for $3,000 at 10% interest. Since this first loan, she's been back a couple of times to fund a new web site and grow her business.[4]

Visit the Prosper site to read other stories like this one. Earlier in this chapter, I suggested that these loans were "right-sized" for Main Street businesses. I think this story is a great example of how sometimes it doesn't take much to keep a small business growing and thriving.

▨ **Note** Typical terms for unsecured peer-to-peer loans vary, but you should treat them as short-term financing options. You can expect interest rates from 6–7%, up to 35% or more, and terms from 1 to 5 years.

Borrowing from Mom and Dad or Your Rich Uncle Fred

Borrowing from mom and dad isn't a peer-to-peer loan in the same sense, but I put it in the same category. Some people lump it into what's been called the three Fs—friends, family, and fools. People have been borrowing money from their rich uncle Fred, a very successful old college roommate, or mom and dad since there were rich uncles, college roommates, and moms and dads.

Most of the time it's a young entrepreneur's startup that is the recipient of all the good will, but most of the time these "loans" aren't repaid and should be considered more like a gift. Unfortunately, many small businesses fail, even those started by entrepreneurs with great parents and great ideas. That makes it difficult for the nephew/niece, friend, or child to repay the loan.

---

[4]http://www.prosper.com/community/stories/lara.aspx

Most of the time, it starts with generous parents (or other fool?) saying, "We believe in your idea. You can start making payments to us once you get profitable." It devolves into avoiding Thanksgiving dinner and skipping out on family parties when two years becomes five and everyone loses track of the last time they saw a payment on "the loan."

I once knew a very talented guy who had an opportunity to purchase a very successful Main Street business. Annual revenues were good, there was a steady flow of repeat customers, and the business was complete with all the equipment it needed to conduct business. The previous owner was even willing to work as an employee to help keep things going. All that was needed was the funding to make it come together.

Because the buyer didn't have a very good track record or credit history, a bank loan was out of the question, but he did have a very successful father-in-law. He found the money he needed to buy the business with a 3F loan. Unfortunately, although he was a very talented guy, his talent wasn't running the business and he eventually ended up walking away. The previous owner had to take it over and try to salvage something from what he thought would be his retirement nest egg. The buyer had to face his father-in-law *and* his wife for squandering the loan from "daddy." This is *not* an uncommon tale.

Of course, there are families who can successfully pull it off. Before he passed away, my father-in-law had a knack for keeping loans to his children "strictly business." This is my advice to anyone considering a 3F loan. Here are some of the things he did, along with a few additional suggestions:

- *Create an agreement.* It could be as simple as, "Ty borrowed $1,000 on September 17, 2013, and will pay $100 each month without interest for 10 months." My father-in-law kept a ledger and made a monthly accounting. There was no question in anyone's mind that the "loan" was an actual loan. There was an expectation they would be repaid, and for the most part I think they were. That's not to say a more formal document shouldn't be prepared. In the case of larger amounts, something more formal probably should be drawn up. I have a close friend with family members who, over the years, borrowed from aging parents, basically decimating their assets and estate. Even though all the siblings knew what happened, because there was nothing to suggest those funds be repaid, the siblings who weren't "borrowing" wound up on the short end of the inheritance stick.

- *Consider putting up collateral.* Although I've not experienced it, there are times when collateral might be part of a 3F loan. I'm not suggesting that asking for collateral is (or isn't) appropriate, but if it's part of the agreement, it needs to be itemized and included in the agreement.

- *Talk to your accountant.* As with any financial transaction, depending on the scope of your 3F loan, there could be tax consequences for the borrower or the lender. Make sure you have a complete understanding of what they are on both sides of the transaction.

- *Is equity involved?* This doesn't necessarily mean that you'll be making your friend or family member a true business partner, but you could be giving them a way to make a profit if you're successful without making regular payments to them. They treat the arrangement like an investment in you and your business, and you treat them like an investor. This is a sticking point for many who borrow from friends or family. In my opinion, it's best to treat this type of financing the same way you would a loan—whether or not Uncle Fred is inclined to take action should you default.

- *Don't take them for granted.* You might not have a formal agreement. You might not offer collateral or equity. But never take a loan for granted. Do your best to treat the loan the same way you would a formal loan from the bank. Something to be repaid, with interest, on time.

It's been said that 3F loans should be considered business financing of last resort. I tend to agree. Borrowing money from family and friends to finance a business idea can put a strain on even the strongest relationships. I've even heard advice that suggests you shouldn't borrow from friends and family unless you are willing to walk away and never see them again. Definitely not something to be taken lightly, and not something I recommend.

Summary

According to Pepperdine University's quarterly private Capital Access Index[5] for the second quarter of 2013, 44% of the small businesses surveyed turned to family and friends to finance their small businesses. What's more, although that was listed as number five behind going to the bank, business credit cards, personal credit cards, and a personal loan—71% of those surveyed (number one on the list) found success there, well ahead of all the other capital sources mentioned.

Particularly for early-stage, small startups, peer-to-peer lending has the potential to make capital available to many small business owners who have no other options. The next chapter covers the financing designed to help small business owners purchase an existing business.

---

[5]http://bschool.pepperdine.edu/appliedresearch/research/pcmsurvey/pca-index/

Business Acquisition Loans

When You Need Money Now

Many entrepreneurs, including a lot of Main Street business types, opt to purchase an existing business rather than build their business from the ground up. As I mentioned earlier, growing up in a family with a small business, there were a lot of conversations around the dinner table about the nature of small business—including the virtues of starting your own business as opposed to buying an established one. Because my dad had been successful at starting his business with nothing but a hope and a prayer (in addition to a pretty hefty second mortgage on our home), he didn't think much of buying an existing business. Although I respect his opinion, my forays into business ownership have included purchasing a business already established with a clientele.

Although buying an existing business isn't all a bed of roses, it can be a wise move in some curcumstances. Once you've identified your tolerance for risk and you know what type of business you want to be in, the following three questions can help you decide how you want to finance the business.

Do You Have Any Experience?

There's no question, starting your own business carries a certain amount of risk. What's more, if you have some technical expertise in your field, but don't have any experience actually running a business, believe me, running a business is much harder than you might think. In fact, if you start your own business from the ground up, you'll likely spend as much time doing the books, dealing with payroll, creating relationships with vendors, and other similar administrative tasks, as you do working in your business.

Purchasing an existing business often enables you to work with the existing owner for a time to learn the ropes. What's more, you don't want to ignore the importance and value of existing vendor and customer relationships—relationships you don't need to build from scratch. You'll likely already have employees, a functioning business plan, a market strategy, insight into current market conditions, and a tutor (the former business owner) who is motivated to make sure the business is a success.

■ **Note**   One of the advantages of buying an existing business is the opportunity to work side by side with the current owner, who can show you the ropes, make introductions, provide wisdom related directly to the business you're buying, and more.

What Kind of Business Are You Looking For?

Are you looking for a business that is strongly identified with your personal brand? Or are you looking for a business that has already built a successful brand? Although this is a book about how to finance a Main Street business, how you approach these questions will make a big difference in how you approach the challenges of financing a new enterprise.

After my dad passed away, my mother sold the family business to one of the employees. During the sale, he bought the inventory at a discount and immediately changed the name. In reality, what he was buying was the nearly 30 years of brand equity my father had created (which could have given the new owner a little bit of a head start). By immediately changing the name, he spent the money to purchase a business and start from scratch all at the same time.

Early in my career, I worked for a Main Street business that had just been purchased by a new owner. I worked with both of them for a couple of years under the name of the old owner, after which the new owner added his name to the marquee after the old owner's name. A few years later, after the old owner completely retired, the new owner renamed the company. He enjoyed several years of postive brand equity created by the old owner while at the same time building his own.

So once again: what kind of business are you looking for?

What Is Your Risk Tolerance?

Although the upfront costs of acquiring an existing business are higher than starting from scratch, the bank is usually much more willing to loan money to an existing business with a successful track record than to a startup with no track record. Remember, time in business is one of the major criteria lenders want to know when considering a small business loan. Basically, this is not only a question of *your* risk tolerance, but also your bank's.

In addition to time in business, lenders will also want to know annual revenues and your projections for the future. It's much easier to demonstrate these projections with an existing business with a history. Even if the business is currently struggling, a smart buyer will have a plan in place to ramp up sales and turn the business around.

What's more, you'll already have employees in place, a predictable cash flow, instant customers, and products on the shelves, thus making your new business much more attractive to a potential lender.

Once you've asked yourself these questions and answered them to your satisfaction, it's time to start looking for ways to finance your business. And yes, you have a few options.

The First 20 to 50 Percent Is On You

Most lenders will expect you to come up with the first 20–50%. Lenders like to see skin in the game. Like my dad, I've always turned to the equity in my home to finance my entrepreneurial ventures. This is also a source of funds should your savings be insufficient.

A 3F loan—family, friends, and fools—can also be a source of funds. Depending on the type of business you're purchasing, you might also look into angel investors. I read just this morning that a lot of the tech millionaires in Silicon Valley have turned to angel investing to put at least some of their cash to work. Of course, most angels invest in ventures they know something about, so if your business is in the Bay Area and happens to be a technology company, you just might be in the right place at the right time.

Regardless of the type of business you plan to purchase, don't be surprised if the lender expects you to show up with some of the cash yourself.

Is the Seller Willing to Finance?

You might be surprised to learn that many sellers are not only willing to offer at least some of the financing, but they prefer it. In the story of my friend shared previously, with the exception of the down payment, the former business owner didn't want the tax consequences of a large lump sum payment. He was looking at future monthly payments as a way to fuel his retirement and distribute the tax burden over the course of a couple of years. Of course, he did a lot of research into who was buying his business—to discover whether he thought the buyer would be successful as well as the buyer's credit worthiness.

I did the same thing, making my payment out of the monthly cash flow generated by the business, in addition to borrowing some of the equity in my home to make the down payment. Having a current, monthly cash flow is one advantage to purchasing an existing business, and I tried to take advantage of it.

▓ **Note**   Current cash flow is one of the big advantages of buying an existing business. If you buy the right business and run it well, it can finance its purchase, and then some.

In addition to borrowing from the owner at what is often a very reasonable interest rate (even if she is able to finance only a portion of the sale), seller financing can sometimes entice other lenders (like the bank) to invest.

The SBA 7(a) Loan Program

Chapter 5 discussed a number of loan programs offered by the SBA[1] (Small Business Administration). The 7(a) loan program is another source of funds the SBA has determined are appropriate to "…assist in the acquistion, operation, or expansion of an existing business."

When you're applying for a 7(a) loan, the same rules exist whether you're purchasing an existing business or starting a new one. Be prepared to spend some time working with your banker. Remember, it's not uncommon to wait several weeks before you even speak with the banker and another several months before the loan is funded. This can definitely throw a monkey wrench into the works, depending upon how anxious the seller is to finalize the sale.

---

[1]http://www.sba.gov/content/use-7a-loan-proceeds

SBA lenders are a good place to turn if you intend to leverage cash flow to pay for the purchase of the business. The SBA looks favorably upon a business changing hands if it has the potential to increase sales and to hire more employees. That's why the SBA encourages financing when the acquisition has enough cash flow to grow the business and cover borrowing costs, even if the deal is low on assets for security.

Banks and Other Financial Institutions

There's no question we are still experiencing a tight financial market, and the smallest businesses are still suffering the most. But there are lenders willing to offer financing to borrowers who can demonstrate:

- A positive cash flow
- Solid management expertise
- Industry expertise
- A good credit history

The key is to look for a lender who currently finances acquistions in your target industry. You may also be able to build a relationship with the bank that the seller uses.

Be aware, too, that alternative lenders have come to fill a niche in financing business acquisitions over the last few years. Some have been covered already, but here's a brief rundown:

- *Asset-based loans:* These are business acquisition loans that can be secured by any available collateral within the business being purchased as well as any collateral the buyer has. This can include structures, inventory, accounts receivable, equipment, and other fixed assets. Loans are typically 65 to 80% of asset value.

- *Equity financing:* Most private equity firms are interested only in multi-million dollar deals. They're typically not on the lookout for a great deal on business with revenues less $2–$3 million. Additionally, if your business has the revenues an equity firm is looking for, they will likely want some control of your business— maybe even as much as 51%. What's more, they also expect a rate of return somewhere in the neighborhood of 25% or more upon the sale of your business. This is not the way to go if you intend to buy the business and pass it down to your kids.

- *Mezzanine financing:* In a nutshell, mezzanine financing is basically a hybrid of debt and equity financing (bank financing and equity financing). As a result, you don't need to give up as much equity—likely around 20%.

Before You Visit the Lender

It's important to have your ducks in a row before you sit across from the loan officer. Be sure you have the answers to these questions when you're ready to ask for financing:

- *How much is the business going to cost?* Don't go to the banker if you don't know. This isn't the type of transaction where you want to test the waters. Make sure you're "all in" before you visit the lender.

- *Is the seller willing to finance any portion of the purchase?* As mentioned earlier, this sometimes will entice other lenders to become part of the deal. When you sit across from the loan officer, he will likely want to know how much the seller is willing to finance along with the terms.

- *Do you have any personal collateral?* Every lender wants to see some skin in the game. Even though the business you're purchasing likely has inventory, equipment, and other fixed assets, the lender sees your collateral as an indication that you won't just walk away if things go south. They may need a lien on your home or other property to act as collateral.

- *Are your ducks in a row?* Complete the loan package outlined in earlier chapters. Don't take shortcuts. Make sure you have a complete application with all the information the lender requires.

- *Have you talked with several lenders?* Don't feel like you're stuck with the first lender to say yes (although I know that's tempting). Make sure you speak with several lenders. Show them your loan package, have them quote terms and an interest rate, and choose the lender who offers you the highest chance of approval and the best terms.

- *Can you follow up with due diligence?* Although it might feel like a pain every time the lender calls with another question about your loan application, be prepared.

Protesting isn't going to help you get the loan you need. Don't fudge or misrepresent anything on your application or on any of the follow-up questions. They'll find out and your loan will be in jeopardy.

Pie in the Sky or the American Dream?

I completely understand the desire to own your own business and buying an existing business is a great way to satisfy that desire. However, there are a few pitfalls to watch out for. I share them here because you must consider these pitfalls before you sign on the dotted line.

- *Make sure your expectations are realistic.* For example, it's not very realistic to purchase a company, manage employees, and satisfy customers as an absentee owner. Make sure you don't put on rose-colored glasses before you jump in with both feet. You need to maintain a practical and balanced perspective.

- *Make sure you ask the right questions.* I'm the first to admit that I don't know what I don't know. If you haven't been through this before, make sure you have a trusted advisor (hopefully someone who has been through this process) to help you ask the right questions and understand the answers. Even if you have been through this before, it's a good idea to get input from someone who isn't as emotionally attached to the idea of buying the business.

- *Don't get emotional.* Don't let your love of any particular business make you sloppy. Make sure your dispassionately look at the core metrics of the potential purchase before you make an offer to buy the business and head over to the bank. If you don't, the bank will. In fact, they will probably do it anyway.

- *Don't trust a handshake.* Make sure it's in writing. I learned this the hard way. It's similar to being hired and promised, "If you do a good job and demonstrate your ability to contribute at a high level, we'll give you a raise down the road." I wonder how many times "down the road" actually comes. The same is true when negotiating the purchase of a business. If it isn't in writing, it doesn't exist.

Tip Don't trust a handshake. Get it in writing. Despite the best of intentions, people sometimes fail to follow through on promises.

- *Trust but verify.* Before you buy any business, make sure the company's financials verify their claims. You might need to hire an accountant to go through everything to verify, but that is money well spent. Don't be in such a hurry that you fail to make sure you're getting what you're buying.

- *Don't succumb to the "paralysis of analysis."* If you have a hard time deciding whether to buy the business, how will you be able to make decisions when you're actually running it? Part of successful business ownership is the ability to make decisions—sometimes even with imperfect or incomplete information.

It's Part of Being a Small Business Owner

Money may be tight and finding the money to purchase a new business isn't the easiest thing in the world. But let's face it, part of being a business owner is finding the capital you need to fund (or purchase) your business. It shouldn't be a surprise that the challenges of finding capital prohibit many would-be entrepreneurs from starting (or buying) their own businesses.

Purchasing an existing business may be easier to finance than starting from scratch, but it isn't for the impatient or the faint hearted. Take your time, make sure you know what you're buying, and then head to the bank.

Where Should You Look for a Business Acquisition Loan?

This is one time I recommend a visit to the bank. Prepare your application documents, make sure you have up-to-date financial information, and search for a banker willing to work with you. A community bank located near the area of the business you want to buy is a great place to start. It's a good idea to try to build a relationship with the bank that the seller uses. The seller may even be able to give you a warm introduction.

Don't forget: an SBA guaranteed loan is a great vehicle for purchasing a business, if you qualify.

Standard Terms for a Business Acquisition Loan

Expect to negotiate interest rates and terms, depending upon the amount financed, your credit score, and collateral. Revisit Chapter 4 for more information about the terms and interest rates of traditional financing. You may also want to revisit Chapter 5 to read more about the SBA 7(a) loan program.

Summary

For many, purchasing an existing business as the initial foray into entrepreneurship is a good idea. For others, purchasing an existing small business can prove to be a good strategy for expanding a business. The good news is, there are lenders who focus on helping your business acquisition strategy become a reality.

The next chapter covers a related topic: buying a franchise and finding the financing to do so. As you'll see, there is financing specifically designed to help entrepreneurs purchase franchises.

Franchises

There's a Loan for That

Many entrepreneurs decide to buy a franchise rather than start a new business for a number of reasons. Some of them are more obvious than others, but here are a few of them:

- They can start with a ready-made client base

- The already have brand recognition

- They have a parent company to train them on successful best practices

- They have access to marketing resources they wouldn't have starting from scratch

- The company has a proven business model (or at least they say they do)

If you own or are thinking about purchasing a franchise, one or more of these reasons might be why. Did you know, depending on the franchise, it might also be easier to acquire the financing you need to get things started? Not only does the SBA offer small business loans targeted at franchises, they also offer advice regarding SBA-approved franchises.

Franchises approved by the SBA are business opportunities that have agreements accepted by the SBA. In other words, before you sign on the dotted line, the SBA has reviewed the agreement and it complies with SBA guidelines. If you purchase a franchise on the SBA-approved list, the loan process is quicker and easier. Because the franchise agreement has been preapproved, the loan review process is less complex, allowing you and the lender to focus on the specific aspects of your business plan rather than whether or not the franchise is viable.

> ▒ **Note** Being on the SBA's approved franchiser list doesn't mean the SBA endorses the particular franchise. It simply means that it has reviewed and vetted the franchiser's agreement, making it easier for you to get an SBA loan.

The SBA Approved List

Not being on the approved list doesn't mean a franchise is a bad risk. There are numerous reasons any particular franchise might not be on the list. Some franchises decide that they don't want to be included on the list. If you're interested in a franchise that isn't on the list, you'll probably go through a little more complicated review process, but it doesn't mean an SBA loan is out of the question. In fact, according to the SBA,[1] "Being on or off the list is not an endorsement or indication of quality and profitability, so you should still thoroughly research for your potential franchise opportunity."

What's more, even if your franchise is on the list, an SBA loan isn't a slam dunk. You'll still need to qualify for the loan. The same qualifying standards outlined in Chapter 5 regarding any SBA loan still apply.

Finding an approved francise isn't difficult. In partnership with the SBA, the Franchise Registry[2] publishes a list of approved franchises. You can visit the Registry and search by name to see whether the franchise you're considering is on the list.

If the franchise is on the approved list, in addition to qualifying financially for the loan, you'll still need to identify:

- The purpose of the loan

- The history of the business

- Financial statements for three years (if you're purchasing an existing franchise)

- Aging accounts receivable and payable (if you're purchasing an existing franchise)

- Schedule of term debts (if you're purchasing an existing franchise)

- Projected opening-day balance sheet (for new franchises)

---

[1] http://www.sba.gov/community/blogs/community-blogs/small-business-cents/sba-approved-franchises-how-do-they-work-and-ho
[2] http://www.franchiseregistry.com/index.php

- Lease details
- Amount of investment in the business by the owner(s) (the SBA and the lending institution will still want to see some skin in the game)
- Projections of income, expenses, and cash flow
- Signed personal financial statements
- Personal resume(s) for each of the owners and principals

Once you've decided on the franchise you want to purchase, the SBA suggests the following steps:

- *Make sure you understand the SBA review process.* This will minimize the amount of time it takes to complete the review. If you know what you need to submit and make sure you comply in a timely manner, it makes the process a little easier (this applies to any SBA guaranteed loan).

- *Be prepared.* Make sure you have all the documents needed to process your loan request.

- *Pick a lender.* All across the country there are lenders who regularly work with the SBA and are familiar with the process. You're not required to use a preferred lender, but anything that streamlines the process is a good idea.

Tip Be sure you understand the loan process, whether you're going for an SBA loan or any other type of franchise financing. If you look like you know what you're doing—rather than like a rookie—you'll inspire more confidence in your potential lender.

The SBA's Advice for Picking a Good Franchise

Franchises are regulated by the Federal Trade Commission (FTC), so the government supplies some useful resources and advice designed to help prospective franchisees determine whether they're buying into a legitimate and viable franchise. Even if you don't pursue an SBA loan, they offer good information to help avoid some common scams.

Detailed Disclosure Is the Law

Franchise owners (franchisers) are required to provide you with specific information to help you make an informed decision. It's called the *Federal Trade Commission's Franchise and Business Opportunity Rule.*[3] The franchisor is required to provide a "detailed disclosure document" during the pre-sale stage of your negotiations. It is required to include:

- Contact information for at least 10 previous franchise purchasers in your area

- An audited financial statement

- Executive profile information

- A true view of the business startup and maintenance costs

- An outline of respective franchisee and franchiser responsibilities

They are required to provide this document at least 10 days before you commit to a purchase or exchange any money. They take this seriously enough they have established a hotline should you feel a potential franchiser is being less than forthcoming: 1-877-FTC-HELP.

Make Certain You Do Your Homework

My dad used to say, "Locks are for honest people." In other words, locks won't keep out a crook if he really wants to get in, but they will keep an otherwise honest person from making a mistake if given the opportunity. I think this is true when evaluating a franchise opportunity too. Make sure the franchiser you're about to deal with is truthful in how it reprepresents itself.

- *The disclosure document:* Make sure you read it and understand it. Call all 10 of the references. If you can meet with them in person, even if you have to travel to do so, it's well worth the effort. Compare their responses to what was included in the disclosure document.

- *Investigate success stories:* The franchisor will likely insist that you can be as successful as you want to be. If they identify success stories on their web site or within their promotional materials, follow up. Do some detective work. Make sure the stories they're telling are the real stories of franchise owners.

---

[3]http://business.ftc.gov/selected-industries/franchises-and-business-opportunities

- *Shop around:* You'll learn a lot by investigating several franchises. Reviewing several opportunities will help you make an informed decision about which franchise is right for you.

- *Don't give in to a high-pressure sales pitch:* The FTC requires a seller to wait at least 10 business days after giving you the required documents before making an agreement. Use those 10 days to make sure the franchise is right for you.

- *Compare the contract to the sales pitch:* The SBA's advice? "Don't sign any contract that doesn't mirror the promises that have been made to you at the pre-sale pitch." Verbal and contractual promises should be *exactly* the same.

- *Don't forget your attorney:* All the better if she is experienced with franchise law. It might cost a little more up front, but having a professional who is paid to protect your interests is a smart idea.

Financing Options Outside of the SBA

The SBA isn't the only place to look to finance your franchise; there are other options you might want to consider, depending on the amount of cash you need and your current financial condition.

- *Traditional financing:* If you have a great credit rating, collateral, some cash of your own, and a strong business plan, a traditional term loan isn't out of the question. The guidelines for application required by the SBA are still a good place to begin. Remember, your local banker will want to see how you plan to mitigate risk, so make sure your business plan is convincing.

- *Retirement funds:* Some companies will help you roll your 401k or other retirement funds into a business loan. In my opinion, this should be a financing vehicle of last resort, but there are no financial penalties associated with this type of financing. In other words, this can be a legal use of a retirement account and therefore won't result in financial penalties, but you should consult your tax advisor to see if it is appropriate in your particular situation.

- *Leverage your home equity:* You're basically putting up your home as collateral if you choose to finance your franchise purchase this way, but this is not an uncommon way for many small business owners to get started.

- *Alternative financing:* There are also non-bank financing options available if you look online. Like other alternative financing, the application process is a little easier and loan approvals are a little quicker. You might pay a few percentage points more though, so make sure you investigate all your options.

- *Franchiser financing:* Many franchisers offer financing or partner with lenders who are familiar with their franchise, making the process a little easier. If the franchise you're considering offers financing, and you qualify, this could be the easiest way to get started.

Bankers like brand names. Remember, bankers are generally risk averse. Depending upon the franchise, the brand's reputation, and the number of franchisees around the country, franchises can be easier (or more difficult) to get funding for.

STANDARD TERMS FOR A FRANCHISE ACQUISTION LOAN

Expect to negotiate interest rates and terms depending upon the amount financed, your credit score, and collateral. Revisit Chapter 4 for more information about the terms and interest rates of traditional financing. You may also want to revisit Chapter 5 to read more about the SBA 7(a) loan program as well as visit **SBA.gov** to read more about their franchise loan program.

Avoid These Franchise Funding Mistakes

Here are a few financing mistakes that many would-be franchise owners make:

- *You get impatient:* You've done your research, you've picked the franchise you want to buy, and you may have even met with a lender. Don't let your emotions overcome you. You need to make sure the financing is as right as the franchise.

- *Your financial house isn't in order:* Even if the last few years have been good to you, now is not the time to go out and buy the new car or a cabin in the woods. Make sure your credit report is accurate and up to date. Make sure you know your credit score and are ready to explain anything negative.

- *You don't avoid unnecessary credit purchases:* Every time you purchase a big-ticket item on credit, a credit check is run. If this happens too often, it negatively reflects on your credit report. While you're working to obtain financing to buy your franchise (or any small business loan for that matter), avoid any unnecessary purchases that require a credit check.

- *You don't avoid risky options:* Like other small business financing, there are many options—your local bank isn't the only place to get a loan. Some are more expensive than others and some are downright sketchy. Make sure you've done your homework before you jump in with both feet. The SBA's list of approved franchises is a great place to start, even if you aren't going to seek an SBA loan.

Tip Investigate the franchiser's own loan program. If you're a good credit risk, you might find speedy approval. And the terms might be slightly easier to negotiate. The franchiser, after all, wants you to succeed.

Where Should You Look for a Loan to Purchase a Franchise?

This is one time I recommend a visit to the bank and the SBA program. Prepare your application documents, make sure you have up-to-date finanical information, investigate whether they are on the SBA's approved franchise list, carefully review the disclosure document all that franchises are required to give you, and search for a banker willing to work with you. A community bank near the business you want to buy is a great place to start.

Summary

Purchasing a franchise is many entrepreneurs' entrée into small business ownership. And, many Main Street businesses just happen to be franchises. Because there are loan products specifically designed to finance the purchase of a franchise, it's often a little easier to access the capital you need to get up and running.

The next chapter covers funding a startup, one of the most challenging types of businesses to fund—regardless of the industry. Startup funding is not for the faint of heart.

CHAPTER

16

Startup Funding
Crawl, Walk, Run!

One of the biggest challenges facing most budding entrepreneurs is finding enough capital to get things rolling. Finding a lender willing to fund an untested business model or an untested entrepreneur is a challenge. Although there are funds available for starting new businesses, finding the money may consist of a combination of the options mentioned in this book.

The Cold, Hard Facts

Finding the money to fund your startup isn't easy. It's even tough for the sexiest of the sexy tech companies with incredibly scalable business models. The successful startups that get funding from an angel or venture firm get talked about in the news, but there are many more who aren't able to successfully woo an equity investor. The CEOs who are successful spend countless hours building presentations, searching for likely equity investors, pitching their young companies, and finding an investor who believes in them. The truth is, *nothing* is easy about startup funding—including equity funding.

Even if you recognize that equity funding is not a possibility for your business (which is true for 98% of Main Street businesses), most people headed to the bank around the corner soon realize their local banker isn't interested in helping your "great idea" get off the ground either. Many Main Street businesses get startup funding the same way I did, my father did, and many of my friends did—they turn to the equity in their home or they bootstrap it until the startup starts making money.

Funding a startup takes creativity. In fact some entrepreneurs, in industries like construction, landscaping, or similar businesses are able to fund an enterprise with sweat equity. Although this might not work for a high-tech firm, it's common practice in many industries for established business owners to help new business owners "work" their way into the purchase of an existing business or get a new start.

■ **Tip**   If you've come to the conclusion that your local bank is not going to fund your startup, it's time to get creative. If you have a good idea, you persist, and you broaden your view of what constitutes a funding source, you will find the money you need to get a business off the ground.

One Way or Another, You Need to Have a Little to Make a Little More

If there's a common theme throughout this book, it's the four things every lender wants to know:

- Your credit rating

- Your time in business

- Your annual revenues

- Your collateral

It's true that some lenders weigh some of this criteria differently than others, and even though they are willing to provide a loan if you have less than stellar credit, there are extra costs associated with it. Some lenders may be less concerned about a 550 credit rating than others, but the borrower makes up for it with a few years in business and a strong cash flow of credit card receipts or accounts receivable. What the borrower lacks in credit rating he makes up for in collateral (the credit card receipts or AR). Even then, an MCA (merchant cash advance) lender wants to see a year or two in business. Without a predictable monthly volume of credit card transactions, this isn't an avenue you can turn to.

It's a Lot Like the NBA

I remember watching the 1986 NBA Slam Dunk Champion Anthony "Spud" Web wow the crowd and win the title against guys much bigger than he. At five foot seven, Webb was a very unlikely professional basketball player, let alone a superstar. Nevertheless, even Spud Webb *never* started as center for the Atlanta Hawks.

There are entrepreneurs who are able to successfully start, build, and thrive without the need of any financing, but it isn't easy. Over the years I've known a number of small business owners who were able to build a business without financing. They start slow, maybe even have another job, and build the business over time. But starting a business from scratch, at least one that achieves significant revenues in just a few years, is a lot like asking a five foot seven guy to start as center for the Lakers. He's probably gonna get creamed, no matter how talented he is.

Finding capital to fuel growth or fund working cashflow is one of the skills a successful entrepreneur needs to have. Spud may have made it in the NBA, but he's the only guy that small I've ever seen in my lifetime do it. In some circles, the ability to find capital is considered the cost of entrance into the entrepreneurial game.

What's Your Personal Credit Score?

If you don't know, you need to know.

For any startup, every lender is going to make their initial assessment of your business credit worthiness based upon your personal credit worthiness. In fact, even if you've been around for a few years, many lenders will still insist upon a personal guarantee. In other words, if your business fails to meet its obligations, they expect you to take those obligations on personally. Consider it another way lenders expect you to have skin in the game.

This can work to your benefit if you have a pretty good credit score (680 or higher). Although you might not be able to convince a bank or other lender to fund your idea-stage startup, you might be able to secure a loan, obtain a credit card, or find other financing based upon your personal credit. The challenge is to make sure that you can meet those *personal* credit obligations—otherwise you'll not only have a nonexistent business credit score, but your personal score will be damaged, making it even harder to acquire the money you need to run your business.

That's one of the reasons small business lenders want visibility into your annual revenues. If there are no revenues, you need to demonstrate another way you are going to meet your obligation to the lender. No revenues usually means no way to repay the loan.

Passion for Your Idea Just Isn't Enough

My entire life, I've heard well meaning people suggest that following your passion is the way to be successful. Unforntuately, I'm not convinced that's very good advice. It takes a lot more than passion to run a successful business and sometimes the search to find your "passion" can even handicap an entrepreneur.

Brian Cohen, Chairman of The New York Angels,[1] said:

> Launching a business is about applying good business principles, finding what problems there are for disruption in the marketplace, applying innovative solutions, and—this may be the critical step—executing flawlessly. The quest for passion hurts students when it stops them from taking action simply because they are unsure of their passion. Some more pertinent questions are: Is there a need in the marketplace? Can I actually meet that need? What do I need to learn to implement those ideas into action?[2]

As suggested by Mr. Cohen, I'm convinced the most successful small businesses see an unmet need in the marketplace and develop a product or service to meet the need. It's true, many of them have a passion for what they're doing, but meeting a marketplace need with a product customers and potential customers are willing to pay for is the pathway to financing most startups—passion just isn't enough.

One more question every new business owner should ask is, "Can I put together the money I'll need to get through the first few years and help my business grow after that?"

Speaking from experience, it's a lot easier said than done. What's more, I'm not ashamed to admit I had to shut the doors on a business once because I just wasn't able to find enough capital to keep it going. I started the business by leveraging some equity in my home and personal credit cards (like many Main Street business owners). Unfortunately, because I was unaware of other financing options available to me at the time, when my personal credit was maxed out, and my savings was long gone, I was forced to close up shop, let three people go, and start looking for a job.

Now, years later, there are a number of things I would have done differently. For starters, I would have paid more attention to the financing needs of my young company.

---

[1] http://newyorkangels.com/index.html
[2] http://www.lendio.com/blog/follow-passionor/

▓ **Note**   When you start a business, think deeply about your long-term funding needs on a regular basis. Identify the kind of money you'll need at startup, a year down the road, five years, ten years, and so on. Reality will probably not reflect your projections, but it's good to get in the habit of anticipating your needs.

When You Need More Money to Start than You Have Personal Credit

You're not alone. There are many startup entrepreneurs just like you.

In recent years, many startups turn to *crowdfunding*. If you're not familiar with the concept yet, you will be. The Internet is a hotbed of crowdfunding platforms. The traditional crowdfunding model solicits donations to an idea in exchange for access to the eventual product, such as a T-shirt. Some of these platforms focus on a particular geography while others focus on particular industries. Some are interested in any type of startup. Social networks are also starting to get into the mix, giving entrepreneurs even greater access to potential investors.

Although crowdfunding sites like Kickstarter[3] (probably the best known crowdfunding site) have been around for a while, newer sites are making it possible for investors to trade equity, much like an angel or venture firm, for an investment in your company.[4] Of course, that means you will have dozens, if not hundreds, of investors in your fledgling startup.

Most experts agree that making it easier for startups to raise capital this way will increase the amount of capital available for entrepreneurs. Although I've not personally invested in or received investment from a crowdfunding source, I believe almost anything that helps early-stage entrepreneurs is a good thing. Although I don't believe it will change the failure rate of young companies, I'm convinced we need to throw as much spaghetti against the wall as possible, realizing that small business success is often a numbers game. Small businesses will likely continue to fail, but if there is capital that allows more businesses to start, the net gain will be more small business successes.

---

[3] http://www.kickstarter.com/
[4] The regulations that allow entrepreneurs to sell equity or debt through crowdfunding sites have not been finalized as of the writing of this book, but the U.S. Securities and Exchange Commission is expected to have them in place by the end of 2013. Be sure to get knowledgeable advice before embarking on this path—there are many rules you will need to pay strict attention to.

Other Sources of Funding

I've mentioned bootstrapping and tapping into your home equity. Here are some other sources worth considering if you're looking for cash to get your startup off the ground. I'll admit, some are more attractive than others.

- *Friends and family*: According to Pepperdine University's Second Quarter Private Capital Index report for 2013,[5] 71% of the small business owners turned to the "three Fs" for capital in the second quarter of this year.

  You read about friends, family, and fools in Chapter 13. When all other sources of capital lead to a dead end, this is a source of capital for many entrepreneurs.

- *Small business grants*: As much bad press as the president seems to get regarding his commitment to helping small businesses, the Obama administration's initiative to encourage alternative energy sources and other technology provides grants for small businesses in that industry.[6] Grants associated with other industries or geographic regions may be highly specialized, but if you happen to be in that industry or happen to be starting your business in an area where business development grants are available, it could be a source of capital. That's not to say it's an easy source of capital. Be prepared to jump through some hoops.

- *Incubators*: Companies, universities, or other entities provide everything from laboratories, office space, consulting, cash, and marketing in exchange for equity in your companies. Like any equity investor, you'll be giving up a portion of ownership and profits down the road should your business go public or be sold. Incubators are more likely to be interested in technology startups and less likely to invest in a new barbershop.

---

[5]http://bschool.pepperdine.edu/appliedresearch/research/pcmsurvey/pca-index/
[6]http://energy.gov/public-services/funding-opportunities

- *Bartering:* I know what you're thinking, but then again, maybe it's my own personal bias when considering bartering a legitimate way to fund a small business. However, that same Pepperdine study revealed that 57% of small business owners use trade credit to finance their small businesses, so I guess it's a legitimate funding option after all. A strategic partner within your market might have an interest in helping your startup and even provide funding.

- *Major customer funding:* Depending upon the industry, some customers are willing to invest in a young startup if it means they have access to your products before anyone else in the market. This also gives them some control over your product development, production process, and dedicated support. Many large companies even look to their customers to fund new projects.

■ **Tip**   When all else fails, turn to friends and family for help funding your business. Nearly three quarters of all founders do. But keep your eyes wide open and understand that failure to repay can cause rifts that never heal.

Avoiding the Startup Funding Pitfalls

Because startup funding is difficult for even the savviest entrepreneurs, you have to make sure all your ducks are in a row before you hit the streets looking for money.

- *Don't look for money with a half-baked business plan.* There's no substitute for a well-reasoned business plan when looking for startup cash. Treat startup funding the same way you approach the bank. Build a compelling package that will convince any potential investor that your startup idea isn't a whim, but a thoughtful approach to the market.

- *Don't ignore management.* It's easy to get wrapped up in the idea and spend all your time talking about your wonderful new product. You also need to make sure you have all the players needed to make your idea a *profitable* reality. Investors want to know that you'll be able to execute your idea and make a profit. They want to know who you'll have in place to help make it happen.

- *Make sure you ask for enough money.* The vast majority of great ideas fail because they run out of capital. Look at the worst-case scenario for your capital needs and try to fund that.

- *Get an attorney.* Every investor will want to reap the rewards of their investment just like every banker wants to make interest. Make sure any agreement you have with every investor is accompanied with a legal document covering the terms.

- *Cash flow is king.* Beware the temptation to blow through your seed capital too quickly, and make sure you're paying close attention to your payables and receivables. I've found out the hard way that once receivables aged past 60 days most—if not all—of the profit was gone. Investors expect you to stay on top of that part of your startup.

Startup funding is not easy. In fact, it's tough enough to keep many hopeful entrepreneurs from starting a new business in the first place. If you've been smart with your personal credit, have done your homework, and are willing to think outside the box, you just might be able to find the cash you need to get your great idea off the ground.

Summary

This chapter covered the challenges associated with financing a startup. You read about many of the options available for finding funds for starting a new business. It's definitely not for the faint of heart.

This next chapter discusses the options for finding funds during a crisis.

Crisis Borrowing

Help!

Growing up in a small business family, the ups and downs of my Dad's business was a regular topic of conversation around the dinner table. It didn't help that my Mom worked in the business and that, as a teenager, I drove the delivery truck and worked in the warehouse. As I got older, I started working on the road as an outside salesman. My dad often expressed the opinion, "The only time the bank seems interested in lending me money is when I don't need it."

With the exception of the SBA's disaster loans, which are available for small businesses in the aftermath of a declared disaster, there really isn't much help for a struggling company in the midst of a crisis. If it feels like your banker is unwilling to stick her neck out to help in your time of need, you're probably right. Remember, your banker is risk averse and isn't going to be excited about throwing good money after bad. In fact, if he senses that you are in serious trouble, you might get a notice that your loan is due right now.

The best time to plan for a disaster is before the disaster.

■ **Tip** Don't count on your banker to bail you out when you are in the midst of a cash crunch, especially if it appears they would be throwing good money after bad. Bankers are not in the bailing business. Do your best to identify possible sources of cash for surviving an emergency—*before* you need the money.

Slow and Steady Wins the Race

I love the story of the tortoise and the hare. Just in case you're unfamiliar with this famous Aesop fable, I'll share it here:

> The once was a very speedy hare who always boasted about how fast he could run. Tired of his constant bragging, a tortoise challenged him to a race.

> Thinking the tortoise would be no match for his speed, the hare accepted.

> Not long after the race began, the hare (well ahead of the tortoise) stopped for a nap. While he slept, the tortoise crept by. Just as the tortoise was about to cross the finish line the hare awoke, but it was too late.

> After that the hare had to admit it wasn't his speed but rather slow and steady that won the race.

It's far too easy to put off crisis planning or ignore potential risks when things seem to be smooth sailing. However, that's the time to do it.

Responding to a Small Business Financial Crisis

I can't think of a single small business owner I've spoken to who wants to think about having setbacks resulting in a serious financial crunch. However, if you haven't thought about what you'd do in such a situation, and instead wait until you are in the middle of a crisis, it might be too late.

I recently spoke to a very savvy woman who's successfully been at the helm of her construction-related business for over 20 years. When I asked her what she thought made her successful, I don't think she even took a breath before she responded, "I had a business plan that addressed good times and bad."

I couldn't help but admire her thoughtful approach. Because she had no illusions regarding the likelihood that her business would go through good times and bad, she gave serious thought as to how her company would prepare for bad times. Much like saving for a rainy day, her company set aside funds each month to bolster revenue if income took a temporary dip—regardless of the reason.

When a crisis happens, here are a couple of suggestions that might help your business survive the setback.

- *Take an honest look at the situation.* Sometimes things aren't as dark as they appear. Most of the time, a financial setback is a temporary situation. You may need to adjust your spending priorities and access any capital set aside for such a situation, but take some time to regroup and dispassionately analyze the situation.

- *Activate your plan.* If you've given the situation advance thought and included those thoughts in a business plan, activate the plan. If you haven't created a business plan that includes disaster planning, you'll need to create one. The immediate concern is to fill the gap left by the lost income. If you haven't put aside any capital for such an event, you might need to explore other financing options. The trick is to accurately evaluate whether you expect this to be a temporary setback or a long-term challenge. Temporary setbacks can often be overcome by reducing spending, where long-term challenges force some pretty tough decisions. For most small business owners, it's tough to finance your way out of a long-term financial crisis.

- *Determine your financial priorities.* Start by categorizing your expenses on a scale from "Can't do without it" to "We can survive without it." Anything in the second category should be cut immediately. I know one small business owner who, upon the death of a key partner—about the same time the economy came to a grinding halt in 2008—waited too long to let go of employees the company couldn't afford and didn't need during the recession. Instead, he spent their reserves on "We can survive without it" projects to keep the staff busy. Eventually, it was obvious they needed to reduce staff, but it was too late. They had spent their reserve funds keeping employees they couldn't afford busy instead of keeping the business alive. After almost 40 years, they eventually had to shut the doors.

- *Be flexible.* A financial crisis will often force you to make decisions you wouldn't otherwise make. Sometimes you need to set new goals, commit to doing whatever it takes, and readjust your expectations.

Disaster Loans

You read about the SBA's disaster loans in Chapter 5. If your financial crisis is the result of a declared disaster, such as Hurricane Sandy, which took place in the fall of 2012, the SBA provides low interest loans that assist small businesses that have experienced physical damage due to the disaster. There are also loans for businesses experiencing economic injury in the aftermath of a disaster. You can learn all about government help for businesses hit by a disaster here:

http://www.sba.gov/category/navigation-structure/loans-grants/small-business-loans/disaster-loans

Other Disaster Financing Options

If you have a good relationship and track record with your banker, she might make some capital available, but remember, bankers won't throw good money after bad. Before you talk to the banker, make sure you're prepared to explain how you will turn your financial situation around. "We're going to go out and sell more," might not be enough. You need to convince your banker that your current situation is a temporary setback that can be remedied with the extra time a small business loan may afford.

Unfortunately, most businesses in 2008 and 2009 quickly discovered that there just wasn't capital available, following the meltdown in the financial sector and the beginning of the Great Recession.

You may need to access your personal lines of credit—your home equity or your credit cards. Even if you've been in business for several years, depending on your industry and the nature of the crisis, you may find yourself "untouchable." Small business financing organizations are still digging out of the mess created by events of the last four or five years.

▨ **Note** Bankers may work with you to bridge capital shortfalls if they believe you can get on your feet again. It'll help if you have a new win to bolster your case—such as a major new client, a big order, and so on.

Have You Considered Throwing in the Towel?

There comes a time when the unthinkable decision is the only one left. Having had to close a business myself, I understand how difficult it is to announce to your employees your intention to close the doors. I don't think I'm unique when I say that I stuck it out much longer than I probably should have.

About that time, one of my sons gave me a picture of Abraham Lincoln I still have hanging up in my home office. Lincoln endured a steady stream of failure, before he was elected president of the United States:

1832 Lost his job and was defeated in a bid for the state legislature

1833 His business failed

1835 His sweetheart passed away

1836 He had a nervous breakdown

1838 He was defeated in a bid to become speaker in the Illinois House of Representatives

1843 He was defeated in his nomination for Congress

1848 He was defeated in a bid for U.S. Senate

1856 He was defeated as a candidate for vice president of the United States

1858 Again defeated in a bid for the U.S. Senate

1860 He was elected president of the United States

I've always admired President Lincoln—his ability to bounce back after defeat has inspired me for many years. Although allowing a business to give up the ghost is never easy, it isn't the end. There are countless stories of highly successful entrepreneurs who did the same.

Summary

Previously you read about how financing a startup is likely the most difficult funding challenge a small business will have. In reality, it's even more difficult to finance your business in the midst of a crisis. My grandmother always talked about setting something aside for a rainy day. She canned vegetables, put up fruit, and stocked the shelves of her fruit cellar every summer in preparation for the winter months—and the rainy day. The most savvy small business owners do the same thing.

The next chapter talks about the unique opportunities for funding a woman-owned business.

WOSB and Other Loans

It's No Longer a Man's World

Former SBA Administrator Karen Mills suggested in March of 2012,[1] "Today, women-owned businesses are the fastest-growing segment of new businesses in our economy."

Citing analysis conducted by American Express, Mills said, "[T]he number of women-owned businesses has risen by 200,000 over the past year alone, which is equivalent to just under 550 new women-owned firms created each day."

What was almost exclusively the domain of men seems to be changing. Not long ago I had the opportunity to speak with two very successful women who have been in business for over 20 years. One owns what many people consider a stereotypically woman-owned business—a dance studio. The other woman operates a business that would more likely be identified with men. She runs an industrial sign manufacturing company.

Both women have been in business for over 20 years, and I consider them successful. Having survived the Great Recession strong and healthy, I'd call them wildly successful.

---

[1] http://www.sba.gov/community/blogs/women%E2%80%99s-history-month-bright-future-women-owned-small-businesses

As I talked with these women about the challenges they've faced over the last 20 years, there were many similarities in their stories. This is despite the fact that their backgrounds and the nature of their businesses are different. Both graduated from college and both have experienced the challenges associated with finding capital. Like many small businesses, the dance studio was initially capitalized with home equity. "Originally, the bank didn't take me very seriously," she said. "The only way I could find capital was to get a second mortgage on my home."

Capitalizing the sign company, although challenging, was a little easier because this owner had some mentors and partners who helped bolster her credibility. Over the last 20 years, both businesses have found it easier to obtain the capital they've needed. That's due in part because of the strength of their individual businesses, but also because the attitude toward a woman-owned business is different today than it was 20 years ago. Writes Mills[2]:

> As Administrator of the U.S. Small Business Administration (SBA), I travel all around the country meeting with small business owners and entrepreneurs. I see how their businesses are transforming their industries and rebuilding their communities following the economic downturn.

> These are businesses like UEC Electronics in South Carolina. Rebecca Ufkes, an engineer and the company's president, is laser focused on growing her successful electronics manufacturing business. She is supplying products to major manufacturers, such as Boeing, Cummins Engine Co, as well as the U.S. Marines and Air Force. And she is creating good American manufacturing jobs in the process.

> UEC employs 194 workers, an increase of 49 percent since August 2011. And Rebecca is part of a growing American supply chain of innovative small businesses that is driving large multinational manufacturers to bring more production back to the U.S.

The days when companies like UEC were exclusively the domain of men is fast coming to an end. Lenders are starting to appreciate the fact. That doesn't necessarily mean that lenders are falling all over themselves to lend to women-owned businesses, but then again, acquiring capital is a challenge for any Main Street business owner. However, the SBA has made more than $12 billion available to women-owned businesses through 35,000 or more loans to women-owned businesses since President Obama took office.

---

[2]http://www.sba.gov/administrator/7387?page=2

As discussed, the SBA is not a lender, but they do guarantee what is arguably the largest pool of capital available for women-owned businesses. With that in mind, the SBA's definition of what makes a woman-owned business is probably the best place to start.

What Is a Woman-Owned Business?

As you might expect, the SBA is pretty specific when it comes to identifying exactly what is a woman-owned business and what is not.[3]

> *Women-owned small business concern means a small business concern—(a) which is at least 51 percent owned by one or more women; or, in the case of any publicly owned business, at least 51 percent of the stock of which is owned by one or more women; and (b) whose management and daily business operations are controlled by one or more women.*

—Federal Acquisition Regulations (FAR), Part 19.001 Definitions

SBA Guaranteed Financing for Women-Owned Businesses

Although the federal government does not offer grants to women (and minorities) for funding a business, through their loan guarantee program they help fund many women-owned businesses. The SBA claims that SBA-backed loans to women- or minority-owned businesses are three to five times more likely than other bank loans. Your local SBA office[4] is a great place to find a certified lender in your area who can help you through the SBA process.

Other Resources for Woman-Owned Businesses

In addition to the SBA, there are other avenues for women entrepreneurs. Here are just a few:

- *The Women's Funding Network:*[5] This network matches women seeking funding with investors and interested parties to provide capital. Members of the network invest about $65 million annually.

---

[3]http://www.sba.gov/content/how-does-federal-government-define-women-owned-small-business
[4]http://www.sba.gov/tools/local-assistance/districtoffices
[5]http://www.womensfundingnetwork.org/

- *The Ada Project for Women:*[6] Like most grants, many of these are earmarked for specific industries. This grant is oriented for women in computer science. The group offers fellowships, scholarships, conferences, and other opportunities to network.

- *Grants.gov:*[7] Although the federal government does not offer grants specifically to women, they can't discriminate either. This site lists several governmental grants with a searchable database.

- *American Association of University Women:*[8] The AAUW's goal is to help women get ahead in areas where they are underrepresented, such as business ownership. This organization does not offer specific loans or grant programs for women starting in business, but helps a potential women get a higher education and provide funding for graduates at crucial times during their careers.

This list is by no means comprehensive, and a Google search reveals millions of other likely links. Lest you start thinking the "free?" money associated with a grant trumps a small business loan from the bank, you might want to consider that such grants are not easy to come by—at least not any easier than a loan. There are numerous options for obtaining financing. Were I a woman entrepreneur, the success rate claimed by the SBA would be appealing to me. Nevertheless, you will still need to qualify with the same basic credit requirements found in Chapter 5 of this book and delineated on the SBA web site.[9]

■ **Tip** The Georgia Tech Procurement Assistance center maintains a blog that tracks government related, women-owned small business news (http://gtpac.org/tag/wosb/). Take a look every so often for news that might help you get the funding—or government contracts—you need to succeed in business.

---

[6]http://women.cs.cmu.edu/ada/
[7]http://www.grants.gov/web/grants/home.html;jsessionid=TBJlSLmdZT83
pr2TTYfz6n3lQMXJDQjTTvgbtsz2WhDsp9qvghwj
[8]http://www.aauw.org/
[9]www.sba.gov

Minority-Owned Businesses

The SBA's 8(a) Business Development program can help qualifying minority-owned businesses develop and grow their companies through a number of services that include counseling, training workshops, management, and technical guidance. Although the 8(a) program isn't intended to certify minority-owned businesses generally, it does certify businesses considered to be socially and economically disadvantaged under its nine-year 8(a) Development Program.

This is not a loan program, but it does provide access to government contracting opportunities, which amounted to $18.4 billion in 2010.

It shouldn't be surprising that minority-owned business owners, like every other Main Street business owner, struggle finding the capital they need. The Minority Business Development Agency,[10] part of the U.S. Department of Commerce, provides a number of resources that include access to contracts, capital, and other tools to help minority business owners.

To help minority business owners find the capital they need, they have MBDA Business Centers[11] all over the country. These centers offer financial counseling to help minority-owned businesses grow.

The MBDA doesn't provide loans or grants, but rather provides grants to the Minority Business Centers mentioned previously. The Business Centers provide consulting and financial assistance to minority-owned firms.

Alternative Funding for Women-Owned and Minority-Owned Businesses

Alternative-funding sources like MCA loans, factoring, and peer-to-peer financing offer strong alternatives to bank loans. Savvy business owners who qualify can follow some of the advice mentioned here as well as tap into the resources provided by the SBA and the MBDA to help them better prepare for their chat with a lender. In my opinion, anything that improves your odds is a good thing.

---

[10]http://www.mbda.gov/
[11]http://www.mbda.gov/businesscenters

Summary

This chapter covered the funding options available for women entrepreneurs. In recent years, more and more women have been starting and very successfully running their own businesses—some in industries that have traditionally been considered the domain of men.

In the next chapter, which is the final chapter, you'll learn why small business is so important to the American economy and why access to capital is so important.

Small Business

The Backbone of America

There are nearly 30 million small businesses in this country—six million of them with 20 or fewer employees. These are the businesses you and I identify with when we think of small businesses. It's where we all go to buy groceries, gas up our cars, get a haircut, and have our shirts pressed. When politicians want to talk about small business, these are the folks they talk about. I think it's past time they stopped talking about how important these businesses are to our economy and started doing something to help them. Writes Gary Belsky:

> The [SBA] defines a loan to small business as any business loan of $1 million or less. So a $1.1 million loan to a chain of dry cleaners with $5 million in revenues doesn't get counted, while a $500,000 loan to a 150-worker auto parts wholesaler does.[1]

Is it any wonder it's so hard for anyone, including small business owners, to understand what the politicians are talking about when they talk about small business?

Washington does understand (or at least they should) the value of Main Street businesses. According to the SBA, "Today, there are more than 28 million small businesses in the United States, and those firms create two out of every three net new jobs and employ half of America's workforce."[2]

---

[1]Let's Stop Praising Small Business—and Fund More, Gary Belsky, TIME Business, August 6, 2012
[2]http://articles.washingtonpost.com/2013-04-16/business/38570592_1_main-street-businesses-sba-administrator-karen-mills-sole-proprietorships

> ▨ **Note** Small businesses in the United States create two out of every three new jobs. They deserve more attention—and more capital—from financial institutions and from the government.

What's a Small Business?

The definition of what constitutes a small business is somewhat convoluted in my opinion. You learned about the confusing definition of a small business in Chapter 1. I agree with Karen Mills, speaking as administrator of the SBA, "[W]hen you dive into the data, you see that not all small businesses are the same."

She continued, "Some are startups that are poised to revolutionize their industries. Others are innovative small suppliers that make large corporations more productive. There are also Main Street businesses that are critical to our communities and the sole proprietors who have used their experiences to launch their own firms."[3]

Each of the groups Administrator Mills identifies as small businesses— sole proprietorships, Main Street businesses, high-growth businesses, and suppliers—all have different capital needs and can't be dumped into the same bucket or lumped into the same category. If the country is really interested in job growth, I think it's time to start investing in the very companies Mills identifies as the biggest job creators.

Unfortunately, It Isn't Happening

At the end of the second quarter of 2013, the National Small Business Association (NSBA) released its 2013 Mid-Year Economic Report.[4] One of the data points applies to the discussion regarding Main Street and the challenge associated with finding the capital those business owners need to create jobs and fuel local economies:

> *Today, just two-thirds of small businesses (65 percent) report they are able to obtain adequate financing, down from 73 percent six months ago.*

The report also suggests that many business owners may be feeling more confident about the economy generally, but they don't see a positive outlook for their own businesses.

---

[3]http://www.washingtonpost.com/business/on-small-business/new-blog-series-with-sbas-karen-mills-who-are-americas-job-creators/2013/04/16/8bdcde40-a634-11e2-a8e2-5b98cb59187f_story.html
[4]http://www.nsba.biz/wp-content/uploads/2013/08/2013-MY-Report.pdf

Forty percent of survey respondents have fewer than five employees and 66% of respondents report 19 employees or fewer. The vast majority sound like the Main Street-type businesses this book was written for. The inability of these businesses—the very businesses that are the real job creators in this country—to find the capital they need to thrive and grow is something we need to pay attention to if we expect to create jobs and grow local communities. Sixty-five percent just isn't enough.

The report authors also point out, "Small business plays a huge role in economic growth, specifically when it comes to hiring. Unfortunately, just 18% report increasing their employee size, while 26% report decreases in employee size, resulting in negative net employee growth."

I believe a failure of the system to help small business doesn't look good for job growth down the road. However, for the smallest small businesses, the challenge of finding capital isn't a new phenomenon.

We Need to Stop Blaming the Recession—It Was Only Part of the Problem

Not too long ago the Cleveland Federal Reserve[5] published a paper suggesting, among other things, that small businesses would continue to struggle to find the capital they need for at least the foreseeable future.

Please don't interpret what I'm about to say as an indictment against banks in general, because it isn't. I just don't think we can ignore the fact that traditional small business lending is in decline and many small business owners can't turn to the local community bank for a small business loan. What's more—as much as the recent recession did to exacerbate the situation—it looks like there has been a steady decline in small business lending since 1995.

> *Recent declines in small business lending also reflect longer-term trends in financial markets. Banks have been exiting the small business loan market for over a decade. This realignment has led to a decline in the share of small business loans in a bank's portfolios.*
>
> *The 15-year long consolidation of the banking industry has reduced the number of small banks, which are more likely to lend to small businesses. Moreover, increased competition in the banking sector has led bankers to move toward bigger, more profitable loans. That has meant a decline in small business loans, which are less profitable (because they are banker-time intensive, are more difficult to automate, have higher costs to underwrite and service, and are more difficult to securitize).*

---

[5]http://www.clevelandfed.org/research/commentary/2013/2013-10.cfm?utm_source=August+20%2C+2013+CRPM&utm_campaign=082412+AM&utm_medium=email

In a nutshell, there are fewer community banks and many bankers are moving upstream to potentially bigger and more lucrative fish. The financial crisis caused by the Great Recession hasn't done anything to help the plight of Main Street business owners looking for capital, but the climate that exists today didn't start there.

There Is Hope, One Lender at a Time

The focus of this book has been to highlight the options small business owners have to finance their businesses when the bank says no, but that doesn't mean there isn't hope at the bank. Not too long ago I met with the vice president of a local community bank to talk about what they were doing differently than other banks to help the small business owners in their community. We both agreed the lifeblood of every community is the health and strength of local small businesses.

Her bank doesn't have a national footprint. In fact, they don't even have multiple branches; they are a single branch within a very defined community. You should also know they are that way by design, and have been since 1974. Their mission is to serve their local community, which is still their mission today.

Note Small community lenders in many towns are doing a great job responding to the capital needs of local businesses. The problem is, not every community has such a bank. Thanks to consolidation, larger regional banks, who could step up to serve small businesses, instead have their eyes set on larger firms and the more lucrative loans they can make in the mid-sized sector.

For nearly 40 years, the bank's small business lending focus has been real estate-backed loans, and they've become known for that expertise. In recent years, they started making more traditional SBA-backed small business loans within the 7(a) program. When I asked what they were doing differently from other 7(a) lenders in the area, she said, "We work with a lot of small business owners who have good, healthy businesses, but aren't perfect. They might not meet the restrictive standard of norms and requirements set by bigger small business lenders in our area, but they have proven to be great small business loan customers."

When I asked her to be more specific about their approach, she said there were four key items they look for when targeting customers:

- *Character and history.* The last few years have been tough for everyone on Main Street. If you're in a business that hasn't felt the pinch, consider yourself very fortunate. Because this banker wants to help the businesses in her community, even those who have less than perfect credit, she looks at the management team, whether the business is now current with their monthly obligations, if they have a good product, how competitive they are their market, and so forth. Sometimes these indicators can mitigate a less-than-perfect credit history.

  "If there's a good management team and these other factors are in place, we can make a case to the lending board that the business is a good candidate for a loan," she said. "Of course there is a credit score threshold we won't go below, but we want to make sure we're doing the best we can for all the small businesses in our community."

- *Appreciation for what it's like to be a small business.* "Main Street business customers are what we've built our business on," she said. "Although we do a lot of bigger loans, I'm just as happy to help the small business owner who is looking for a $50,000 loan. To a lot of the Main Street businesses in our community, that's a big loan. We understand what it's like to be the little guy—in some respects, we're the little guy too."

  Processing the paperwork for a $50,000 loan is just as cumbersome and costly to the bank as with a $500,000 loan. It's hard to argue against the logic of avoiding the smaller loan amounts. Unfortunately, Main Street isn't often looking for anything more. In fact, my experience at Lendio[6] is relevant here. Of the thousands of small business owners who visit the web site every month, 59% are looking for loans of $50,000 or less. As long as regulations make it unprofitable to lend to Main Street, the banking industry isn't going to do it. Streamlining the process for what the SBA considers micro-loans (loans of less than $50,000) would be a good start.

---

[6]http://www.lendio.com

- *The documentation burden of small business lending.* It's not uncommon for the months-long approval process to take its toll on a small business owner. What's more, "most banks are six weeks out before they'll even talk to you about an SBA loan," says our community banker. "Instead of sending the 20-page packet to the borrower and wishing them luck, I try to meet with potential borrowers right away. Instead of expecting the small business owner to plow through a bunch of unfamiliar documents, I digest their financial statements and other documents and start the SBA forms myself. That way, the next time we meet, we can fill in the blanks and try to shorten a very lengthy approval process."

- *Community lending decisions are made in the community.* Of course this is problematic for bigger banks, but the approval process begins and ends within the walls of a single branch. Everyone involved in the lending process is under one roof, part of the same team, and invested in helping the small business community in *their* community. Although this particular community bank is on the smaller end of the small business lending continuum, I think they're on to something. It reminds me of what it was like when our banker took this kind of interest in us—he was familiar with our industry, he knew my partners and myself, and he liked to do business at our office. When we needed cash, he made it happen.

I think this is a great example of what community banks all over the country should be doing to encourage small business growth. Before our conversation ended, she shared a great example of what their bank is doing differently. She described a member of their lending board who wasn't very positive about a small business loan to a local restaurant. In fact, he was going to vote against the loan.

Before the vote, he decided that it didn't make sense to vote against the restaurant until he had eaten there. After his visit to the restaurant, he became one of its biggest advocates. Because he made the extra effort to see for himself, the less-than-perfect potential borrower (if measured exclusively by credit score, time in business, and collateral) gave him another data point to mitigate some of the potential risk, enabling the bank to make the loan.

It's Really Sad When Even Small Business Advocates Don't Get It

Early in September of 2013, Ray Hennessey, the editorial director of Entrepreneur.com, a popular source of information for small business owners all around the country, blithely suggested, "It's high time to eliminate the SBA altogether."[7]

I wish I could say that Hennessey was alone in this opinion. As I speak and write about this topic, there are many in certain sectors of the business community who remind me that they agree with him.

I *don't* happen to be one of them.

I agree that there are problems at the SBA. I just don't think throwing the baby out with the bath water is a good idea. Hennessey suggests, "The SBA's loan programs are designed to fund businesses that can't find funding elsewhere." He suggests private equity and venture firms raise billions of dollars to fund the *good* ideas.

I'm not sure what Hennessey is thinking. As you read about earlier in this book, only a very small percentage of small businesses (even fewer Main Street businesses) are likely to have a scalable-enough model to interest a private investor or venture firm. It seems naïve to suggest that a new dry cleaner or hardware store would have any luck convincing a venture firm to invest in its business.

The SBA, banks, and other small business-focused lenders fill an important niche to the very businesses you and I consider small.

It sounds like Hennessey is suggesting that any business that isn't interesting to a private equity investor or venture firm is a bad business?

Mr. Hennessey does point out that lumping sexy tech startups, Main Street businesses, and larger small businesses into the same category just doesn't make sense. Nevertheless, labeling the company that presses my shirts as unworthy of credit because a venture firm is likely uninterested in funding their company is kind of shortsighted.

The SBA does have some problems, but guaranteeing (remember, it's local banks that really do the lending) too much capital to Main Street doesn't happen to be one of them. The smallest small businesses are still struggling for capital as banks remain anxious about lending to them. Does that imply they are bad companies or their ideas are bad ideas? Heavens no. It does suggest that the way we approach lending to Main Street needs to be re-evaluated to better serve that segment of the small business borrower market.

---

[7]http://www.entrepreneur.com/article/228186

Mr. Hennessey suggests the SBA has a horrible track record and funds risky ventures. He may have missed Deborah Gage's piece in the *Wall Street Journal*[8] late in 2012. "[T]here is evidence that venture-backed start-ups fail at far higher numbers than the rate the industry usually cites," she says. "About three-quarters of venture-backed firms in the United States don't return investors' capital, according to recent research by Shikhar Ghosh, a senior lecturer at Harvard Business School."

Note   Bad loans are the bane of every lender, from the local bank to the richest venture fund. Regardless of rigorous pre-loan due diligence, a large percentage of businesses will fail no matter who lends the money. And private equity and venture capital firms are not as adept as they think at picking the winners.

Although venture capitalists like to laud their success rates, "The National Venture Capital Association estimates that 25 to 30% of venture-backed businesses fail," she writes.

What's more, the likelihood the average small business would be interesting to an equity investor is only around 2%. They just don't have the potential to scale big enough to make investors interested in the rate of return.

If there's a problem with small business lending, it's the definition of what we call small businesses. I've spent my entire career working in small business. I've worked in a Main Street business with fewer than five employees, along with a software company with almost $30 million in revenues and more than 250 employees, and the venture-backed startup I work at now. They are all categorized as "small businesses" but have very different capitalization needs.

I don't know how anyone can suggest that banks aren't facing risks and are making bad decisions with money backed by the SBA when the success rate of venture capitalists and other equity investors isn't much to sing and dance about. Some startups fail. There's not much we can do about that, regardless of how much research we've done into their potential viability. I'm not convinced it's irresponsible bankers foisting bad loans onto the SBA. I think it's just a part of the same small business environment that causes 35% of venture-backed businesses to fail, too.

Hennessey also writes, "[The SBA is] not as important as you think." He argues, "In short, large businesses, in industries that matter most, get only a negligible amount of funding from SBA-backed loans. That means shutting

---

[8]http://online.wsj.com/article/SB10000872396390443720204578004980476
429190.html

down the program would have a negligible effect on lending. Why keep a government agency in place if most of the market wouldn't notice it is gone?"

Main Street is what keeps communities alive, where most of U.S. jobs exist, and where most jobs are created. Based on the sheer number of employers, then, the majority of the market would in fact notice if the SBA disappeared.

If anything, I think the SBA should be encouraging the banks within its system to step up and make more loans to Main Street business owners. They could do this by streamlining the process for loans of less than $50,000, for starters. Big businesses in major industries don't need the SBA, that's true. What's more, the SBA wasn't created to help big business. It's the businesses you and I rely on to fix our cars, provide childcare to our children, and do our dry cleaning.

There Are No Easy Answers

Although there are community banks all over America that are anxious to lend to small business, alternative lenders who are making capital available to thousands of small business owners who need the cash to grow and thrive, and equity investment for the lucky few who qualify, we're a long way from getting the job done. Unfortunately, there's no easy answer either.

It is time for politicians on both sides of the aisle to come to the table with ideas that will help the very entrepreneurs that are most likely to fuel the economy. Hopefully, there will come a time when there won't be a need for a book like this.

Until then, don't take "no" from your banker as a legitimate answer. You have options.

Index

Get the eBook for only $10!

Now you can take the weightless companion with you anywhere, anytime. Your purchase of this book entitles you to 3 electronic versions for only $10.

his Apress title will prove so indispensible that you'll want to carry it with ou everywhere, which is why we are offering the eBook in 3 formats for nly $10 if you have already purchased the print book.

:onvenient and fully searchable, the PDF version enables you to easily nd and copy code—or perform examples by quickly toggling between istructions and   applications. The MOBI format is ideal for your Kindle, hile the ePUB can be utilized on a variety of mobile devices.

;o to www.apress.com/promo/tendollars to purchase your companion Book.

Other Apress Business Titles You Will Find Useful

Due Diligence and the Business Transaction
Berkman
978-1-4302-5086-9

Exporting
Delaney
978-1-4302-5791-2

Improving Profit
Cleland
978-1-4302-6307-4

Tax Insight
Murdock
978-1-4302-6310-4

Tax Strategies for the Small Business Owner
Fox
978-1-4302-4842-2

Healthcare, Insurance, and You
Zamosky
978-1-4302-4953-5

Know and Grow the Value of Your Business
McDaniel
978-1-4302-4785-2

Advanced Social Media Marketing
Funk
978-1-4302-4407-3

How to Recruit and Hire Great Software Engineers
McCuller
978-1-4302-4917-7

Available at www.apress.com

CPSIA information can be obtained at www.ICGtesting.com
Printed in the USA
LVOW13s0124151113

361403LV00003B/110/P